Motorbooks Performance Handbook Series

HONDA PERFORMANCE HANDBOOK

Glenn Marston

Motorbooks International
Publishers & Wholesalers
®

First published in 1990 by Motorbooks International Publishers & Wholesalers, P O Box 2, 729 Prospect Avenue, Osceola, WI 54020 USA

© Glenn Marston, 1990

Library of Congress Cataloging-in-Publication Data
Marston, Glenn.
    Honda/Acura performance handbook / Glenn Marston.
       p.   cm.
    ISBN 0-87938-387-9
    1. Honda automobile—Modification.   2. Acura automobile—
    Modification.   I. Title.   II. Series
    TL215.H58M37 1990   89-13174
    629.28′722—dc20   CIP

On the front cover: The 1984 Honda CRX autocrosser run by Memphis, Tennessee, racer Grady Wood, Jr., in the C Street Prepared class. The car's engine is from a CRX Si, but uses dual 40 DCOE Weber carburetors. Tuning help from CRE/Performance. *Glenn Marston*
On the back cover: The King Motorsports/Mugen tube-frame CRX road racer driven by Jim Dentici won the 1989 SCCA GT-3 class. High-style Integra: Jackson Racing's body kit, Dragon wheels and ventilated brake discs. *Jackson Racing.* Oscar Jackson, founder of Jackson Racing, right, works on a high-performance Honda engine. Author Glenn Marston at speed in his 1974 Civic 1200 autocrosser.

Printed and bound in the United States of America

To my wife Carol for her patience and assistance, and to my mother and father for inspiring my interest in reading and writing

---

Contents

Acknowledgments

Thanks to the following for their help in gathering information: American Honda Motor Co. Inc., A-T Engineering, Corky Bell of Cartech Inc., CRE/Performance, HKS USA Inc., Jackson Racing, King Motorsports, RC Engineering, Dave Jenkins of Rubin Postaer and Associates, Shankle Automotive Engineering Inc.

Preface

I was not surprised when Motorbooks International asked Glenn Marston to write a book about Honda performance upgrades. I wasn't surprised in their choice of authors or their choice of titles.

Honda was the first in this country to really make the transition from practical mundane Japanese economy car into performance and styling leader. This transition was completed not only with the aforementioned but with unequaled build quality.

Ten years ago most people scoffed at Honda aftermarket tuning pioneers like Oscar Jackson. People wondered why he and others were wasting their time and their talents with mundane cars like the Honda. Now Oscar and his competitors are in an enviable position. They now make parts for some of the hottest and best selling performance cars sold in America.

I've known Glenn Marston for many years. When I started *Grassroots Motorsports* magazine five years ago I turned to Glenn Marston as my very first writer. Yes, Glenn has been an editor for the magazine since its inception. I turned to Glenn because he shared my passion for tinkering with old sports cars. Glenn understood what I was trying to create in my new magazine. Glenn also has a great deal of writing and organizational talent. In fact, he is managing editor of one of Florida's most successful newspapers.

I guess I'm partially responsible for getting Glenn so involved with Hondas. As part of a deal on a truck I sold, I took a battered, well-worn 1973 Civic in trade. Since Glenn was having constant reliability problems with his Opel race car at the time I asked Glenn if he would like to reincarnate the little Honda into an Improved Touring race car and Street-prepared race car. Having owned another Honda used strictly as transportation he realized that the little Civic would probably be a better race car than his old Opel.

I guess the rest is history. The staff at Motorbooks International were impressed when they saw the project car stories in *Grassroots Motorsports* and after checking Glenn's credentials asked him if he would write this book.

I'm glad to be a part of it and hope you enjoy it enough to get into amateur racing of one type or another with your Honda.

Tim Suddard

1

Performance—a matter of principle

With the Civic, CRX, Prelude, Accord and Integra, Honda and its Acura subsidiary have earned a reputation for building stylish, high-performance cars that are economical both to buy and maintain. Rarely does an automobile company produce success story after success story the way Honda has without strong leadership and clear goals. So it should be no surprise that Honda uses the following company principle to guide its operations: "Maintaining an international viewpoint, we are dedicated to supplying products of the highest efficiency at a reasonable price for worldwide customer satisfaction."

While such a guideline could easily be an outgrowth of Honda's recent triumphs, this company principle preceded today's delivery of high performance, economy and quality by more than thirty years. The policy was set in 1956, merely ten years after Honda was established as a company to convert small wartime communications engines into motorized bicycle engines, and six years before Honda

The first model imported to the United States by Honda was the N–600. Commonly called the Honda 600 or Honda sedan, it was sold from 1970 through 1972. The car was powered by a 600 cc two-cylinder, air-cooled engine.

became an auto manufacturer. History reveals few cars that can link success to such concise goals; for instance, the Ford Model T and Volkswagen Beetle on the basis of simplicity and value, and Ferrari and Porsche for performance. And it may be that only Honda has been able to meet all three of these goals at once.

The heart of Honda

The elements of Honda's company principle can be traced directly to its founders—Soichiro Honda, who gave the firm its name and headed engineering, and Takeo Fujisawa, who headed sales and business operations.

The performance element is clear from the thinking of Honda himself. His personal philosophy—as reported by Japanese writer Tetsuo Sakiya in *Honda Motor: the Men, the Management, the Machines*—is this: "Life is short, but by achieving greater speeds a man can make his life a little longer and more affluent."

Honda put this idea to practice as soon as he had the resources. As a mechanic in Tokyo in the mid 1920s, Honda became a racer by driving a car he built in his spare time. He constructed the race car from scratch except for its eight-liter Curtis-Wright V–8 aircraft engine.

Honda was born in 1906 in Komyo Village, Japan. His father was a blacksmith who also repaired bicycles. Inspired by this and machinery of all sorts, Honda moved to Tokyo in 1922 to become an apprentice mechanic for the Art Shokai garage. He learned his trade for six years, and in 1928 gained the owner's permission to open an Art Shokai branch in another city, Hamamatsu.

There he continued racing, experimenting with offset engines and supercharging. The supercharging necessitated improvements in cooling and valve seats which Honda devised. In July 1936 Honda completed a new racer and entered it in a contest called the All-Japan Speed Rally, held on the edge of Tokyo. Honda was leading as he approached the finish line, only to have a slower car cut him off. The cars crashed and rolled over three times, throwing Honda out. The wreck crushed the left side of his face, dislocated his shoulder, broke his wrist and ended his racing career. His brother, a passenger in the car, was also seriously injured.

The next year Honda embarked on a new venture: manufacturing. He hoped to perfect a die-cast iron piston ring and established a company, Tokai Seiki Heavy Industry, to do so. Honda knew a bit about casting as he had earned a patent for a wheel

with cast-iron spokes. However, he couldn't get the hang of casting piston rings. Honda became a recluse, slaving away at a solution. Neighboring foundries would not help him solve the riddle, so Honda finally enrolled as a part-time student in the Hamamatsu High School of Technology. There he learned that a lack of silicon in the iron alloy was robbing the rings of elasticity. Nine months after first trying, Honda perfected his cast piston ring. He quickly built this technique into a thriving business.

World War II brought Honda prominence, allowing him to enlarge his casting and machining business and expand it into other fields. But the war eventually brought his downfall, as it would for the country as a whole. Toyota bought forty percent of Tokai Seiki in 1941. Then the war brought more piston ring business to the company as it supplied parts and machines for aircraft and naval engines. As the war progressed, Honda invented automated machines to manufacture piston rings because many of Tokai Seiki's skilled workers were drafted into the military. Honda's greatest contribution to the Japanese war effort, however, was an automated process for producing airplane propellers. The Honda method turned out a pair of propellers in thirty minutes, whereas previous hand methods took as long as a week to yield a single propeller.

When Japan surrendered to end World War II, Honda showed—as his namesake company showed again decades later—that the right frame of mind can ease the worst of problems. While many of his countrymen sank into depression, Honda sold the remainder of Tokai Seiki to Toyota and spent a portion of the proceeds on a barrel of medical alcohol. With this he made whiskey and spent a year partying with friends.

At the end of the year, though, Honda returned to industry. In 1946 he established the Honda Technical Research Institute, which was later renamed the Honda Motor Company. Honda first used this company to buy World War II communications engines and convert and sell them for use on bicycles. When the supply dried up, he designed his own engines and continued his powered-bicycle business.

Honda, however, wanted to move beyond bicycle engines and sought a financier for his fledgling firm. Through a mutual friend, Honda met Takeo Fujisawa in 1949. Fujisawa, who was born into poverty in Tokyo in 1910, worked his way into industry in the 1930s and by the early months of World War II had established a company to make machine tools.

After the war, like Honda, Fujisawa yearned to re-enter industry, although in his specialty of merchandising rather than engineering. It had been Fujisawa's sales and management abilities that had moved him through the ranks and into business ownership before and during the war—just the opposite of Honda who had thrived on technical skill. When the pair met in 1949, Fujisawa said he could not finance Honda's company personally but vowed to find backers who would. With Honda's acceptance of this pledge, the heart of the Honda Motor Company was formed, a heart that would prove doubly strong because of the two men's vastly different but complementary backgrounds.

Honda explains the dichotomy this way, in Sakiya's *Honda Motor:* "Assuming that reaching the top of Mount Fuji was the ultimate goal, both Fujisawa and I had the same goal. But I took one route while he took another route because he had a different philosophy and personality. If we had been taking the same route, we might both have been finished off by an unexpected storm."

And so developed the philosophy of the Honda Motor Company, Honda knowing that the mountain top could not be reached without the best in engineering, performance and construction technology, and Fujisawa knowing that the summit was unobtainable without attractive technology and satisfied workers whose allegiance would result in well-made products to please customers.

Fujisawa and his managers proved the value of his pathway to success by building sales and employee and customer satisfaction to the point that the company became a model for others to emulate worldwide.

Honda and his engineers proved the worth of his path by winning racing championships and then infusing the technology gained through this research into new designs.

Racing development

The Honda Motor Company first entered international racing as a motorcycle manufacturer. In 1954, Soichiro Honda declared that the company would seek victory in one of the world's most prestigious motorcycle races, the Isle of Man Tourist Trophy. To do so the company first established an intensive research and development program, since his company's engines and components were nowhere near adequate. Among the advancements were flywheels that would not shatter at high speeds, chains that were stronger because they were lighter and the reciprocating forces they placed upon themselves were thus reduced, and—most telling for the future—combustion chamber designs based on intensive testing and experimentation. By researching the basics itself, Honda Motor Company was able to beat the competition by 1961 when it won the first

five places in the 125 cc and 250 cc Tourist Trophy classes.

As the company's interests were moving into automobiles in the 1960s, so were its racing interests. In 1961 Honda bought a Cooper-Climax Formula 1 car. Formula 1—for single-seat, open-wheeled road racing cars—is the top class in international auto racing. At the time, Formula 1 engines were limited to 1500 cc in displacement with no supercharging allowed. The first Honda Formula 1 engine was a V–12 derivation of its 250 cc motorcycle twin. The engines shared 125 cc per cylinder displacements as well as a number of internal components. The four-valve-per-cylinder, double-overhead-camshaft engine used twelve carburetors and could rev to a raucous 14,000 rpm, the noisy exhaust routed through twelve individual exhaust headers. The engine, mounted transversely to a six-speed transaxle, was first raced in Honda's RA-271 car.

The chassis was designed at the last moment by Honda when Lotus of England dropped out of Honda's program three months before the expected debut in 1964. In August 1964 the RA-271 entered its first race, the German Grand Prix, with US sports car racer Ronnie Bucknam at the wheel. That year Honda worked to get the bugs out of the new car and no races were won. In 1965, however, Honda delivered a new RA-272 chassis and hired a second US driver—Richie Ginther—to join Bucknam, speeding along testing and development. Although progress was slow through most of 1965, Ginther's previous Formula 1 experience helped Bucknam, who'd been a Formula 1 newcomer the year before, and the entire team. In the last race of the year, the Mexican Grand Prix, Ginther qualified first and finished first by 2.89 seconds.

This last race of the year was also the final race for the 1500 cc engine size. By this time the Honda engine had been converted to fuel injection and the exhaust had been manifolded into three banks of four pipes. These changes, coupled with elements that still traced their roots to the motorcycle engines, resulted in 230 horsepower at 11,500 rpm with 14,000 rpm still allowable. In 1966, the engine limit was increased to 3000 cc, and Honda competed for three years under these rules. While these cars were at times competitive, they did not win.

For fifteen years Honda stayed out of Formula 1 until it returned in 1983 as an engine maker, supplying the power for the Williams team of England. Williams-Honda won one race in 1984, four in 1985 and nine in 1986, a performance that won Honda its first constructors' championship. Since then, Honda has been the most sought after engine supplier in Formula 1.

Among the benefactors of Honda's first auto racing program were the company's earliest cars, the S-500, S-600 and S-800 sports cars, the N-360 and N-600 sedans, and Z-600 coupes, produced in the 1960s and early 1970s. These models made their marks in Japan with high performance for cars of their caliber. However, their extremely small size and comparatively mediocre acceleration on the stretched-out highways of the United States limited their appeal as imports. The principle was right, though, so once Honda had the capacity to build larger and more sophisticated cars, it infused racing-related features into cars that ordinarily would be intended for family use. Today, Honda is known around the world for its performance and quality.

The most valuable outgrowth of Honda's racing was its mastery of combustion within the engine.

Honda used this ability first to produce more power in its 1950s motorcycle-racing and 1960s auto-racing engines, then to conquer stringent exhaust emission laws in the 1970s, and to provide unparalleled combinations of power and fuel economy in its production engines in the 1980s.

When Honda and Fujisawa retired in 1973, they carried their dedication to the company to the ultimate and at the same time reinforced the principles upon which they founded the Honda Motor Company. They did so by officially renouncing all ownership claims to the company and by cutting traditional ties that would have allowed their sons to succeed them as company leaders. Honda and Fujisawa insisted, just as they did in engineering and production, that all decisions be based on merit. Especially the choosing of their successors.

2

The family tree

While the Civic was not the first Honda automobile sold in the United States when it was introduced in late 1972, it was the company's first serious car. No longer could the words Honda and car be condensed into a single term, Hondacar, meaning a toy-sized caricature of an automobile like the earlier 600 series microcars, and S series sports cars. Outwardly, the Civic was no more than an economy car of the two-box layout then popular. This layout was represented by one compartment or box for the engine, and another for passengers and luggage. But within its light, compact body the Civic contained many extras of the sort that had already brought success in the United States to Japanese auto makers Datsun and Toyota.

Among these features were a four-speed, floor-shifted transaxle; power-assisted front disk brakes; rack-and-pinion steering; an all-aluminum, overhead-camshaft engine; four-wheel independent suspension; reclining bucket seats; and an excellent heating and outside-air ventilation system. Few of the day's sports cars had more to offer, and no economy cars—even the more-for-less Datsuns and Toyotas—could match this line-up. In short, the Civic offered the technical features of a BMW and what has proved to be the durability of a Mercedes, at a Volkswagen price.

The Z–600 shared the N–600 sedan's platform and drive-train, but the 600 coupe had completely different body-work. It was sold in the United States in 1971 and 1972.

The Civic was the first Honda large enough and powerful enough to be saleable in the United States as a mainstream sub-compact car. With a transverse-mounted water-cooled four-cylinder engine, front-wheel-drive, and four-wheel independent suspension, the Civic set the basic mold for nearly all other Hondas to follow.

This first-generation Civic design proved to be the longest lasting, being produced in several variations through 1979, and many of its advantages were retained in the later designs. The second-generation Civic was introduced in the United States as a 1980 model. The third generation was unveiled for the 1984 model year and included the CRX, a two-seater built on the Civic driveline but having its own body. The fourth generation, including a new Civic-based CRX, was introduced as a 1988 model line.

Civic
First generation, 1973–79

The 1973 Civic was sold with an 1170 cc engine, and offered in two-door and three-door body styles. The more common three-door body has a rear hatch and fold-down rear seat, while the two-door has a small trunk lid underneath the rear window. This opening provides access to the spare tire and a small luggage compartment. A pair of external hinges just below the rear window is the most obvious clue to a two-door Civic, which otherwise looks the same as the three-door.

The first Civic is short, low and light—virtues that continue in today's models. A 1973 Civic is 139.76 in. long, 52.95 in. tall and weighs 1,536 lb. in two-door form and 1,552 lb. as a three-door. There is no frame as such, since the car is a unibody design. The sheet metal that forms the body also supports the suspension, steering and drivetrain.

Suspension in the front is by MacPherson struts. At each front wheel a strut attaches to the top of the fender well from the underside. It connects through a needle bearing and a bushing of synthetic rubber, which the other suspension bushings are made from as well. A coil spring works against a cup on the underside of the fender well, and against a collar about halfway down the strut. The bottom of the strut attaches with a sleeve to the suspension upright, also known as the spindle or steering knuckle. The upright is connected to the body in three other ways: by a lateral link, also known as a lower control arm, by a radius rod and by the steering rack's tie rod.

The lateral link is attached to the upright with a ball joint and to the body with a bushing. The link, along with the strut, locates the upright and wheel side to side. The radius rod is welded to the outer end of the lateral link, and angles inward as it runs forward to the front cross-member, where it is attached through a bushing. The radius rod controls wheel movement forward and backward.

The tie rod has a ball joint at each end and attaches with the outer ball joint to a lever on the upright. This lever is also known as a steering arm, and the tie-rod ball joints are also known as tie-rod ends. Left-right movement of the steering rack, in response to turning the steering wheel, results in right-left movement of the wheels. The top of the strut pivots around the needle bearing while the bottom pivots around the lateral link's ball joint. The tie rod's ball joints allow it to follow the vertical and rotational movements of the upright as the car passes over bumps, and steers left and right. The outer tie-rod ball joint is threaded onto the tie rod. The front wheels' toe is adjusted by screwing the tie rods in and out of the outer tie-rod ball joints until the toe specification is met. Looking directly down at the wheels, the wheels are toed in if their fronts point inward; they are toed out if the wheel fronts point outward; if the wheels point directly ahead, there is zero toe. The measurement is made with an alignment gauge.

A small anti-roll bar clamps to the radius rods through a bushing just in front of the lateral links. It is attached to the forward cross-member through a pair of synthetic rubber bushings and U-shaped brackets. The anti-roll bar is a torsion bar, which is a type of spring. Made of heat-treated steel, it resists twisting and springs back to its original shape when pressure on it is released. The bar is twisted when the front of the car leans to one side or the other, or one wheel moves to a different level than the other. It lessens body roll (lean) by exerting an upward force on the side of the car leaning over—the side on the outside of a turn.

The rear suspension is also by MacPherson struts. As with the front suspension, the top of the strut attaches to the underside of the fender well, through a bushing. There is no needle bearing, though, as the rear struts do not rotate. The coil spring works against a cup at the top and a collar on the strut. The strut attaches to the upright with a bracket, and the lateral link attaches to the upright through a pair of bushings, rather than a ball joint, since there is no rotation. The lateral link's inner end attaches to the body with another bushing.

The radius rod is not steeply angled as in the front; it runs almost directly forward. The forward end of the radius rod attaches to the body with a bushing that allows the rod to pivot in a vertical arc. The rearward end of the radius rod passes through an

eyelet-shaped portion of the upright. The rod is threaded where it passes through the eyelet. A nut, washer and conically shaped bushing are sandwiched into each side of the eyelet. The wheel's toe is set by adjusting the position of the bushings forward or backward until the specification is met.

The engine and transaxle sit sideways between the left and right front suspension components. The drive axles link the powertrain to the suspension and wheels, and the left-side axle is longer than the right-side axle. An axle, also known as a driveshaft or halfshaft, has a pair of constant-velocity joints on each end.

A constant-velocity joint, also known as a CV joint, is an advanced type of universal joint. Simple universal joints allow a rotating shaft to move in a single plane—as between the transmission and rear axle of a front-engine, rear-drive car, where they compensate for the rear axle's bumps and dips on uneven roads. Because of its geometry, a simple cross-type universal joint binds and produces an uneven (fast, slow, fast, slow) rotation when a shaft moves in two planes—as between the transaxle and a front wheel, which may turn left or right, and move up or down, at the same time. Constant-velocity joints get their name from their ability to smooth out this pulsation, and must be used when a shaft moves in more than one direction.

Inside a constant-velocity joint are six large ball bearings held in a circle by a cage. They run in a slotted outer race that surrounds the bearings and a slotted inner race that forms the core of the joint. Depending on the joint (inner or outer), one race receives the axle's rotation and the other passes it on. The joint is packed in a special grease and enclosed in a bellows-shaped plastic boot. Only the inner joints

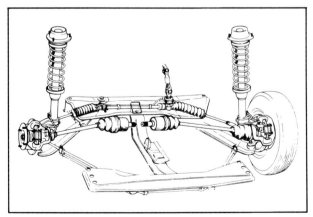

The first-generation Civic's front suspension uses a combination of MacPherson struts, lateral links, forward-running radius rods and a front anti-roll bar.

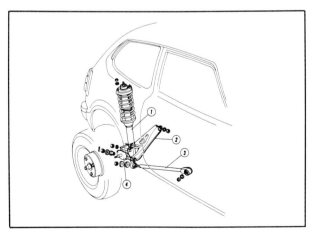

The first-generation Civic's rear suspension uses struts, radius rods and lateral links.

can be disassembled and rebuilt, although boots can be replaced on all the joints.

The four-speed transaxle of the 1973 Civic set the general parameters for four- and five-speed Honda transaxles through the late 1980s. The transaxle combines a four-speed transmission and differential, also known as a final-drive unit, in one compact, lightweight aluminum housing. The gears run in engine oil, which has the advantage of lower drag and easier shifting, compared to the thicker gear oil of conventional front-engine, rear-drive cars.

The transmission gears are laid out much as they would be in a conventional transmission. Nonremovable forward gears are on the mainshaft, also known as the cluster gear, and are integral with the input shaft. The mainshaft gears drive removable forward gears and their synchronizers on the countershaft. Here the difference from a conventional transmission appears: there is no output shaft. Instead, the final-drive pinion gear is on the front of the countershaft and meshes directly with the ring gear on the differential. The final-drive gears are angled spur gears that, unlike the hypoid gears used in most front-engine, rear-drive cars, drive off their outer edges rather than their sides.

The differential allows the front wheels to follow a turn without binding. Since one drive wheel is on the inside of the turn and the other is on the outside, they are traveling on different arcs and thus turning at different speeds. The differential allows this difference in speed. The shortcoming is that it can drive just one wheel at a time; if traction is poor enough and power high enough, the wheel with the least traction will spin while no power goes to the wheel with the most traction. Limited-slip differentials connect both axles through clutches to reduce traction loss while allowing just enough slippage to negotiate turns. These units are available from outside suppliers; Honda has not offered a limited-slip differential.

The transaxle is connected to the engine through a diaphragm-type clutch pressure plate and a single conventional clutch disk. The diaphragm design allows smoother engagement and less resistance through the clutch pedal than other types.

The original Civic engine was out of production by the end of the 1970s, but many of its basic features—even the general appearance of its open-deck aluminum block—were still apparent fifteen years later in the four-valve-per-cylinder engines introduced in the fourth-generation Civic in 1988.

The 1973 Civic engine had a bore of 70 mm and a crankshaft stroke of 76 mm for a displacement of 1170 cc. The bore is the diameter of one cylinder, the stroke is the distance traveled by the piston from one end of the cylinder to the other, and the displacement is the volume that one piston will displace in a single stroke, multiplied by the number of cylinders. The engine produced 52 hp at 5000 rpm and 60.5 lb-ft of torque at 4000 rpm. This led to 0–60 mph acceleration times of 14.1 seconds, and 19.2 seconds at 68 mph from a standing start in the quarter mile. Although the engine was eager and reliable, the early Civic's performance forte was handling, not acceleration. The engine did lend itself to high-performance modifications, however, and the Civic won several road racing championships in full-race trim.

The Civic's engine block is aluminum except for the cylinder liners, which are iron and nonremovable. While most blocks have a closed deck—with just the cylinders, a few bolt holes and a couple of fluid passages breaking the flat, metal surface—the Civic deck is open. The cylinders are cast in pairs and are known as siamesed cylinders because there is no water jacket between them. The junctions of cylinders 1 and 2, and 3 and 4, are solid aluminum. These pairs of cylinders rise from the bottom of the block, unconnected to the surrounding water jacket that makes up the upper portion of the block, and you can look directly down into the water jacket. The piston-to-cylinder-wall clearance is exceptionally tight. The minimum is 0.0012 in. (0.03 mm), and the maximum for used engines is 0.0039 in. (0.10 mm).

The bottom end of the engine is equally unconventional. Rather than having separate main-bearing caps bolted to the block to hold the crankshaft, the Civic engine uses an aluminum girdle. The girdle is, in essence, five main-bearing caps connected by a maze of strengthening ribs. The girdle makes the bottom end rigid, without the added weight of steel main-bearing caps. The oil pump mounts to the girdle, which contains oil passages that route oil to the crankshaft and cylinder head. The passages are also known as oil galleries.

The cylinder head is an aluminum, cross-flow design. In cross-flow heads, the intake ports are on one side and the exhaust ports are on the other. The air-fuel mixture enters on one side of the engine and exits as exhaust gas on the other. This design generally produces more power than one with intake and exhaust ports on the same side of the cylinder head. The faces of both the intake and exhaust ports are round. The combustion chamber is a rounded, hemispherical shape and works with slightly dished pistons to yield a compression ratio of 8.3:1.

The valves are arranged in two rows, one canted toward the intake ports, the other canted toward the exhaust ports. They are operated by rocker arms that work off a centrally mounted overhead camshaft. The camshaft is driven by a toothed belt that runs off the front of the crankshaft. A gear at the middle of the cam meshes with a gear connected to the oil pump shaft; this shaft runs from the cylinder head to the oil pump at the bottom of the block. The cam also runs the distributor (by gear) at the front of the cylinder head and the fuel pump (which has its own cam lobe) at the rear of the cylinder head.

Several changes marked the first-generation Civic, most having to do with the ever-increasing regulations for exhaust emissions and safety. After the Civic had been sold for just one year, larger bumpers were added, and the engine displacement was increased to 1237 cc to compensate for power lost through additional emissions controls. The bumpers increased the car's length from 139.76 to 146.85 in., and its weight from 1,536 to 1,605 lb. for the two-door. For the three-door, the weight went from 1,552 lb. in the first year to 1,621 lb. in the second.

In 1975, Honda unveiled an unusual new engine in the Civic. This new model was called the Civic CVCC for its Compound Vortex Controlled Combustion engine. This updating of the Civic included slight changes in body trim, and a 2.17 in. (65 mm) increase in length in the front fenders to accommodate the larger CVCC engine. Honda continued to offer the 1237 cc model, known thereafter as the Civic 1200, in all parts of the United States except California.

In 1975, with the addition of the CVCC, Honda added a five-door wagon to the Civic line-up. It differed from the hatchbacks by being longer and by using a solid rear axle on leaf springs. The next significant change in the Civic—remember, Honda is infamous for its myriad detail changes—came in 1976 when the front suspension was partially redesigned. On 1976–79 Civics, radius rods are attached to the lateral links by bushings rather than being welded. The radius rod passes through the link, with a bushing on each side, and nut and washer on the backside clamping the rod and bushings in the link.

In 1978, the Civic line was restyled slightly, with improved bumpers being the most obvious difference. These bumpers shortened the Civic about two inches. Also in 1978, the Civic 1200 received a new cylinder head with larger intake and exhaust valves; larger, straighter intake and exhaust ports; and a deeper combustion chamber with domed pistons to match.

CVCC engine

Compound vortex controlled combustion is a method for reducing exhaust emissions with few add-on controls. While Honda veered away from strict use of this high-combustion-turbulence process when the CVCC engine was still experimental, the name stuck. The final process, as put into production in 1975, requires a second intake system that includes an additional carburetor barrel and intake manifold passages. Also required for each cylinder are an additional intake port and valve, and combustion chamber. These three components are called the auxiliary port, auxiliary valve and pre-chamber.

To understand the logic behind the CVCC system, it helps to know a bit about emissions control. There are three parts of exhaust gas that the US government required to be reduced starting in the late 1960s: carbon monoxide, unburned hydrocarbons and oxides of nitrogen. Year after year, beginning in earnest in 1970, the government required cars to emit lower percentages of these components, which contribute greatly to the photochemical smog that blankets car-clogged big cities. California, home of the worst smog problems, has long drawn up its own tougher regulations and preceded federal emission crackdowns by a year or more.

From 1970 through 1974, the federal regulations focused on lowering carbon monoxide and unburned hydrocarbons. This was done mainly by leaning the fuel-air mixture. A lean mixture contains less gasoline for a given amount of air, while a rich mixture contains more gasoline in relation to the air. A rich mixture is easy for a spark plug to ignite, and an engine is tolerant of rich mixtures to an extent, producing nearly as much power as it would with an ideal mixture. Conversely, lean mixtures are more difficult to ignite with a spark, often resulting in misfiring, stalling or overheating. The main advantage of a lean mixture, beyond carbon monoxide and unburned hydrocarbon reduction, is improved fuel economy, an offshoot of the small amount of fuel in the mixture.

With the federal government's clamping down on emissions, the CVCC system became important. Not only was this engine able to run smoothly and cooly on a lean mixture, but a pivotal benefit was its ability to reduce oxides of nitrogen emission at the same time.

Although the average temperature of the CVCC exhaust gas is higher than that of a conventional engine, the peak temperature (at the time of combustion) is lower. Normally, a lean fuel-air mixture increases oxides of nitrogen emission—this was the petrochemical puzzle that led to use of catalytic converters by most car makers in 1975. These two-way converters were used to clean up carbon monoxide and unburned hydrocarbon emissions, but they reduced oxides of nitrogen emission by using rich fuel-air mixtures or exhaust-gas recirculation; both methods reduce combustion temperature. Honda, though, used the CVCC system, which requires fewer add-on components and generally produces greater power and fuel economy.

Honda based this radical new design on the principle that a flame will easily ignite a fuel-air mixture that is too lean to be ignited by a spark. A special three-barrel carburetor was designed to work with this new flame-ignition system—consider it a two-barrel carburetor with a small auxiliary barrel added on. These two main barrels work just like those for the Civic 1200. One is a primary barrel, the other secondary. The primary barrel is used for idling and cruising, while the secondary comes into play at wide throttle openings at high engine speed only. On the 1200, the opening of the secondary barrel is controlled by an additonal throttle plate just above the normal secondary throttle plate. This additional plate, called an air valve, is connected to a counterweighted lever that works to keep it closed, but is not connected to the throttle linkage. When the secondary throttle is open and the flow of air through the carburetor is sufficient to overcome the closing force of the counterweight, the air valve opens. This way, opening of the secondary barrel can be delayed until enough airflow exists to support its use without stumbling or loss of power.

In the CVCC carburetor, there is just one secondary throttle plate. But between it and the throttle linkage is a diaphragm-type servo called the secondary diaphragm. This vacuum mechanism is connected by a small port in the carburetor to the backside of the primary venturi. The venturi sucks fuel into the barrel by creating a vacuum on this backside. The greater the airflow, the greater the vacuum, and thus the amount of fuel sucked into the engine. By porting the secondary diaphragm to this area of vacuum, opening of the secondary barrel is again delayed until airflow can support its use. So, the only practical differences between two main barrels of the two carburetors is that the CVCC carburetor is jetted to produce leaner fuel-air mixtures than the conventional carburetor.

On the other hand, the auxiliary barrel of the CVCC carburetor produces a rich fuel-air mixture. This mixture travels through the auxiliary ports and valves to the pre-chambers. There are three openings to a pre-chamber. The first is to the auxiliary valve. The second is the threaded hole for the spark plug. The third is a short passageway to the main combustion chamber. A moderate mixture, neither rich nor lean, forms where the pre-chamber and the main chamber meet. These three levels of mixture—lean, moderate and rich—are known as charge stratification. The moderate mixture helps ensure firing of the lean main-chamber mixture; the stratification provides a gradual transition from rich to lean and helps prevent misfires. In fact, technically, engines using this combustion process system are known as stratified charge engines.

A single four-stroke cycle of the CVCC combustion system takes place this way:

1. The downward intake stroke of the piston sucks air and fuel through the auxiliary and main barrels of the carburetor simultaneously into the pre-chamber and main combustion chamber.

2. The upward compression stroke of the piston compresses the fuel-air mixtures in both chambers. At roughly 40 to 20 degrees of crankshaft rotation before the piston reaches the top of the cylinder (depending on engine model and speed), the distributor fires the spark plug.

3. The spark ignites the rich pre-chamber mixture and the flame spreads to the moderate mixture where the two chambers meet, and then into the main combustion chamber where the normally hard-to-burn lean mixture ignites and burns thoroughly. The CVCC engine requires more ignition advance than normal because of the increased time of starting the flame in one chamber and spreading it to another. Burning the fuel creates the downward power stroke.

4. Momentum of the flywheel and firing of the other cylinders forces the piston upward once more, this time on the exhaust stroke, completing the four-stroke cycle.

Honda employed the CVCC system through 1987 on most of its carbureted models—the Civic 1200 (1973–79) being an exception. To meet tougher emissions requirements in 1980, Honda added a two-way catalytic converter. But even with the converter, Honda was able to use less intense methods of emission control than others because of the CVCC system's inherent efficiency and cleanliness.

Beyond the cylinder head, the 1975 CVCC engine differed from the 1200 in a number of ways; it was an all-new design. The block, for instance, was made of iron rather than aluminum. But while the cylinder head was still made of the lighter material, the aluminum main-bearing girdle was gone. Instead, the CVCC uses conventional, individual iron main-bearing caps. The CVCC bore is a bit larger at 74 versus 72 mm. And the stroke is much longer at 86.5 versus 76 mm. These bore and stroke measurements yield a displacement of 1488 cc. The new engine made 53 hp at 5000 rpm and 68 lb-ft of torque at

3000 rpm. With power outputs similar to the 1200's, the new CVCC engine produced similar acceleration in the Civic: 0–60 mph in 15 seconds, and the quarter mile in 20.1 seconds at 67 mph.

Although the CVCC pre-chamber system has been applied to three separate Honda engine lines, the engines commonly known as the CVCC are the iron-block models produced for the Civic, Accord and Prelude from 1975 through 1983. They appeared in three displacements: 1488, 1597 and 1751 cc.

In 1975, the engine was unveiled as the 1488 for the Civic. In 1977, the 1597 appeared in the first Accord; its bore was the same as the 1488's but its stroke was lengthened to 93 mm. In 1979, the 1751 appeared first in the Accord and then in the Prelude, which debuted midyear as a 1980 model. For this engine, both the bore and stroke were increased, the bore to 77 mm and the stroke to 94 mm.

Additionally, the bores were located differently in the block, although the block dimensions overall remained the same. In the 1488 and 1597 engines, the distance between cylinders 2 and 3 is greater than between 1 and 2, and 3 and 4. In the 1751, the cylinders are equally spaced. The engine series was marked by a vast array of detail changes throughout its nine-year production span, as detailed in the specification charts.

Accord
First generation, 1977–81

When introduced in 1977, the Accord stunned the automotive world, and most often it was compared to a Mercedes. The body was as rigid and tight as a submarine hull. The controls were ideally located on convenient stalks or on uncluttered portions of the dashboard. The heating and air conditioning systems were fully integrated, and as capable as a Cadillac's. The seats were well-contoured and richly upholstered. And unique small features were included like a covered change box, inside releases for the hood and hatch, and a graphic display to show open doors and alert the driver to other small problems. These little extras had been unheard of in an economy car, even an upper-level model like the Accord. As common as the idea is now, no one produced a subcompact car with luxury-car features until Honda unveiled the Accord.

Mechanically, the 1977 Accord is laid out much like the first Civic. The suspension, for instance, is quite similar. In the front, coil springs surround MacPherson struts which are located on the bottom by lateral links and radius rods. In the rear, they are located by A-arms and radius rods.

The engine is the 1597 cc version of the CVCC powerplant introduced the previous year in the Civic CVCC. It is rated at 68 hp at 5000 rpm and 85 lb-ft of torque at 3000 rpm. In 1979, the Accord received the 1751 cc CVCC engine, rated at 72 hp at 4500 rpm and 94 lb-ft of torque at 3000 rpm. The larger engines were needed because of the size and weight increase over the Civic.

A 1977 Accord is 162.8 in. long, 63.8 in. wide, 52.4 in. tall and weighs 2,045 lb. Performance was average for the day, although the car felt faster than

The original Accord was the first car to offer a full list of sports and luxury features in a modestly priced small car.

This combination of quality and technology set a high standard for all subsequent Hondas.

The 1979 Prelude was Honda's first modern sports coupe. In its first incarnation, however, it was little more than a second-generation Civic with a larger engine and different bodywork.

the numbers indicate. A 1977 Accord accelerated from 0–60 mph in 15.4 seconds and covered a quarter mile in 19.5 seconds at 66.5 mph.

In 1979, a four-door Accord sedan was unveiled along with the 1751 engine, but otherwise the car changed little during its six-year life.

Prelude
First generation, 1980–82

The first Prelude was part of a joint engineering project that resulted not only in Honda's first modern sports coupe but also the second-generation Civic. Both came out of a mid 1970s Honda experimental program, Project NA (NA stood for New Automobile). While three running prototypes were built by Honda Research and Development, the design was not put into production. However, Honda's production engineers wove details from the project into the first Prelude and second Civic, which were built on the same general platform. This means the two cars have similar dimensions and share basic suspension components, although the actual hardware differs enough in detail that it will not interchange.

As with the Civic, a unibody design eliminates the need for a separate frame, and the suspension front and rear is independent and by MacPherson strut. But the newer suspension is simpler than the older. For instance, the Prelude does not use a pair of radius rods to locate the front suspension's lateral links. Instead, a simple U-shaped anti-roll bar is bolted with two brackets and bushings to the front cross-member. The bar's trailing arms (the legs of the U) are bolted with bushings through sleeves in the lateral links. The links and the anti-roll bar's connections through the sleeves are much like those of the 1976–79 Civic, except that radius rods are not used. This simplification was no first; in fact, MacPherson himself designed his first strut suspension this way. But through careful design Honda provided good handling at a lower cost, and with less weight.

The Prelude's rear suspension also eliminated radius rods. However, in this case, they were replaced by stamped steel trailing arms. The front of the arm attaches to the unibody through a bushing and cross bolt. The rear end of the arm is forked and attaches to the upright through a pair of bushings and cross bolts. The inner bolt of this pair has an attached washer that is eccentrically shaped and fits in a well on the trailing arm. By using an alignment gauge and turning the bolt, the toe can be adjusted. A lateral link is attached to the upright and unibody with a bushing each, and the rear suspension is otherwise similar to that of the first-generation Civic. To help tune its handling for sports use, the Prelude has a rear anti-roll bar that neither the first- nor second-generation Civics were produced with.

The Prelude is roughly the same size as the first-generation Accord, although it is a bit heavier. A 1980 Prelude is 161.4 in. long, 63.8 in. wide, 51 in. tall and weighs 2,150 lb. The Prelude is also close in size to the second-generation Civic four-door sedan. Besides bodies, the other difference between the Prelude and the second-generation Civic is the Prelude's

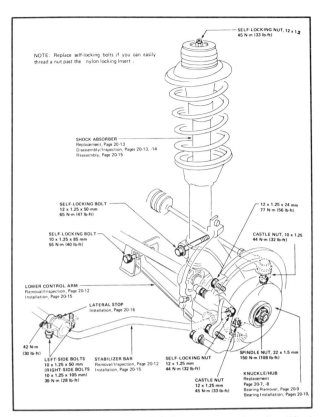

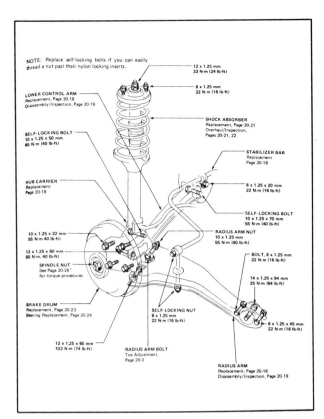

The first-generation Prelude's front suspension simplified the layout used in earlier Hondas by doing away with the radius rods. The front anti-roll bar took on double duty by locating the lateral link fore and aft, making the radius rods unnecessary. This layout was also used on the second-generation Civic.

The first Prelude's rear suspension differs from previous models' as well. A stamped trailing arm replaced the radius rods; this component is also called a radius arm. It was also Honda's first rear suspension to use an anti-roll bar. The same suspension layout, minus the anti-roll bar, was used on the second-generation Civic.

1751 cc CVCC engine. The new engine accelerated the Prelude from 0 to 60 mph in 11.5 seconds and through the quarter mile in 18.7 seconds at 74 mph.

Civic
Second generation, 1980–83

When introduced in 1980, the second-generation Civic was all-new. The styling was a modernized, crisper rendition of the original lines, and the car's dimensions were stretched in all directions except height. The 1980 Civic's length is 148 versus 145.5 in. for the 1979 Civic, and the width is 62.2 versus 59.25 in. The height is close at 53 versus 52.4 in.

The engines were updated as well. The 1237 offered in 1979 grew to a 1335 in 1980. The bore remained the same but the stroke increased from 76 to 82 mm. The 1335 also gained a CVCC-style head, making it the only all-aluminum pre-chamber Honda engine at that time. The iron-block 1488 engine remained, but was thoroughly updated with modified designs for the pre-chamber and main combus-

tion chamber. Both engines were equipped with two-way catalytic converters to meet the ever-toughening emission requirements. The 1488 produced 67 hp at 5000 rpm and 79 lb-ft of torque at 3000 rpm, significant improvements over the original 1975 version. The increased power led to quicker acceleration. The 1980 Civic 1500 GL ran 0–60 mph in 12 seconds, three seconds faster than the original, and covered the quarter mile from rest in 18.4 seconds at 73 mph.

The heart of the original Civic remained, but the soul of the new car was transplanted from the first Accord. While the first-generation Civic was advanced and feature-filled when introduced in the fall of 1972, it was clearly an economy car. Much of the interior was painted metal. Optional air conditioning was more add-on than integrated, the carpeting draped loosely over the floor rather than snuggling tightly into each corner, and the car was loud and a bit rattle-prone. The first Civic was lovable, eager and reliable, but unsophisticated by the end of the decade.

On the outside, the second-generation Civic retained the styling cues of the original version. But inside, it was much closer to the feature-filled Accord.

The second-generation Civic was the first Honda to include a full line of body styles: hatchback, four-door and station wagon.

The credit for upping small-car standards so drastically belongs to the Accord. So, when Honda introduced the second-generation Civic, it had already become famous for its little jewels, and could not fall back on the old ways. The second Civic was so successful at meeting the new standards that, except for styling, it could easily have qualified as the Accord's successor. That was not to happen, however, as the Accord was poised for an expansion into the mid-sized class in 1982. And the Civic had gained a second role—that of bridging the gap between the original, small Accord and the larger version soon to be released.

For the new line of Civics, the two-door sedan was eliminated. The three-door hatchback and the station wagon remained, however, and a four-door sedan was added in 1981. Both the wagon and the four-door sedan rode on longer chassis than the hatchback.

The second-generation Civic had a shorter production life, a philosophy that Honda adopted for subsequent models: update the car after two years on the market and replace it altogether after four years.

The updating in 1982 was subtle but thorough. Metal-faced bumpers were replaced by vinyl-clad bumpers, the instrument panel was completely redesigned and the traditional round headlights were replaced by rectangular units. The changes resulted in a car that was about half an inch longer and about fifty pounds heavier, depending upon the exact model. A sports version, the Civic S, was introduced in 1983 but was largely a cosmetic makeover of the Civic GL, with the 1488 engine and five-speed transaxle.

Accord
Second generation, 1982–85

When Honda introduced the second Accord in 1982, it stepped up a notch in size. In worldwide terminology, the Accord became an intermediate-sized automobile. In the United States, the new Accord was considered a compact, rather than a subcompact as it had been in its first iteration.

With this step up in automotive class, the Accord gained additional refinement. Rather than add more features—the original Accord was so fully

In 1982, the second Accord separated itself from the Civic by moving up in size from subcompact to compact, and by using the substantially larger Prelude engine.

As with the original Accord, the second version was offered as a hatchback or a four-door.

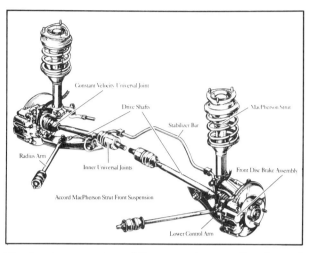

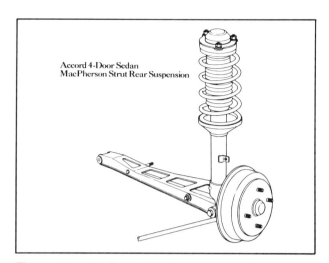

The front suspension of the second-generation Accord differs from the first mainly in location of the anti-roll bar, which was moved behind the suspension.

The rear suspension was again very simple with struts, lateral links and radius rods in the second Accord; the SEi and some hatchbacks received an anti-roll bar.

equipped that its packaging was considered revolutionary for the class—Honda decided simply to make the car work better: More room (length and width) would be added, the car would weigh less to use less fuel and perform better, it would be more aerodynamic for efficiency and quietness, and it would handle better.

The engineers met these goals with typical Honda efficiency. They increased the wheelbase (the distance between the front and rear wheels) by 2.8 in., the overall length by 2.6 in. on the hatchback and 1.7 in. on the four-door and the width by 1.2 in. All this came with a sixty-five-pound reduction in weight (from 2,240 lb. for the 1981 hatchback to 2,175 lb. for the 1982 hatchback), and a reduction in aerodynamic coefficient of drag from 0.48 to 0.41.

The handling was improved by rearranging and fine-tuning the components. In the front, MacPherson struts are connected to the unibody by lateral links and trailing radius rods; the anti-roll bar is behind the suspension and is attached to the links rather than the radius rods as in the first Accord. In the rear, MacPherson struts are located by trailing arms and reversed A-shaped control arms. Coil springs surround the struts, front and rear.

The 1751 cc engine produces 75 hp at 4500 rpm and 96 lb-ft of torque at 3500 rpm. This results in acceleration of 0–60 mph in 13 seconds and through the quarter mile in 18 seconds at 70 mph.

Prelude
Second generation, 1984–87
Until the launch of the 1984 Prelude, Honda had a reputation for fine cars with many convenience features, but not for truly high performance. The second-generation Prelude changed that; it was one of the first front-wheel-drive cars with handling to match that of rear-drive cars. What's more, its acceleration was strong; the second-generation Prelude was the first Honda capable of accelerating 0–60 mph in less than ten seconds (9.7 seconds).

Even more important for Honda was the Prelude's role as a bellwether model—it introduced a number of technical advances that soon appeared in a wide range of other Hondas. For instance, the wedge-shaped styling with low-profile nose and cowl, combined with large windows and a steeply raked windshield became the model for Honda for years to come.

The Prelude's new front suspension layout appeared on the third-generation Accord and Prelude, and the fourth-generation Civic and CRX. Honda describes it as a double wishbone design; that's accurate, but in common terms it's a bit vague. A typical double wishbone suspension uses an upper and a lower control arm. Each is wishbone-shaped; these arms are also called A-arms for their shape. The wide end of each wishbone—the legs of the wishbone or A—is attached to the chassis through bushings and cross bolts, and the pointed end is attached to a short upright through a ball joint. Geometrically, the front suspension of the second-generation Prelude follows this pattern, but mechanically its appearance is nothing like that of a traditional double wishbone suspension.

Each side of the front suspension is made up of a lateral link and forward-reaching radius rod, much as in the first Civic. The only difference is that the radius rod attaches to the link with bolts rather than being welded on. Also attached to the lateral link through a ball joint is the bottom of the upright. The upright stretches high into the fender well, where it connects to a small wishbone through a ball joint. The wishbone is as high as possible on the chassis without hitting the top of the fender. The spring is mounted in a strut-like cup in the top of the fender well; the spring surrounds the shock absorber and passes through the middle of the A-shaped wishbone. A bracket, which splits in a fork-shaped pair of linkages to clear the drive axles, connects the spring and shock absorber to the lateral link. An anti-roll bar wraps around the backside of the engine and transaxle, and is attached to the lateral links.

Honda's double wishbone suspension serves several purposes: it's more compact than most strut layouts, allowing lower fender and hoodlines. It also controls wheel movement more accurately, improving cornering through better tire contact and reducing torque steer, which can make a front-wheel-drive car veer when accelerated hard. The second-generation Prelude rear suspension is essentially the same as that of the second-generation Accord.

The engine is the final example of the second-generation Prelude's growing influence. With all-new 1829 cc design with cast-iron block and aluminum-titanium cylinder head, it was the first of the twelve-valve (three valves per cylinder) Honda engines. The engine itself soon appeared in the Accord as well, and the twelve-valve design appeared a year later in the third-generation Civic and first CRX.

The engine features two intake valves, an auxiliary valve for the CVCC pre-chamber, and an exhaust valve. The new combustion chamber design encourages a much freer flow of air and fuel into the engine, and exhaust out of it. The new intake valves are 35 mm in diameter each, versus 36 mm for the single intake valve of the 1751 engine, and the exhaust valve is 35 mm for the new engine versus 30 mm for the old.

Rather than a single carburetor with a primary, secondary and auxiliary barrel, the 1984 Prelude uses two 34 mm Keihin constant-velocity sidedraft carburetors with an additional fuel atomizer for the CVCC intake tract. While most automotive carburetors are downdraft, meaning that the air enters at the top and exits at the bottom with fuel mixed in, sidedraft carburetors are in effect mounted sideways so that the air enters at the front and moves through sideways to exit as an air-fuel mixture at the back. This allows a straighter path for the mixture to pass through the manifold into the intake ports, eliminating the ninety degree bend of most intake manifolds for downdraft carburetors.

The constant-velocity design of the Prelude's carburetors is also uncommon, found generally on motorcycles or older British cars, but rarely elsewhere. The carburetors are constant-velocity in that a

The second-generation Prelude was Honda's third breakthrough model. Its twelve-valve engine and precise suspension made this a sports coupe that lived up to its good looks.

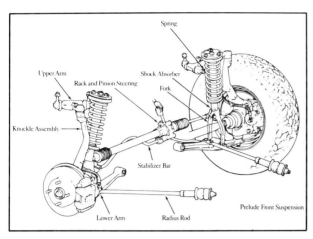

The 1984 Prelude, which made its debut in mid 1983, was the first Honda with the company's now-common double wishbone suspension. Used only on the front of the car, the components don't have the appearance of a conventional double wishbone suspension. But it does have its precise geometry, which is important for good handling.

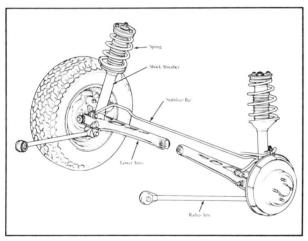

In the rear, the second Prelude uses struts, lateral links, radius rods and an anti-roll bar.

slide forms the carburetor's venturi, and opens or closes in response to airflow. The venturi of a conventional carburetor is the necked-down portion of the barrel on whose backside fuel is introduced. A vacuum is produced at the back edge of the venturi drawing the fuel into the barrel, which is also known as the carburetor throat. By allowing the venturi to shrink at low engine speeds (and thus at low airflow), the fuel mixes with the air more efficiently.

The second-generation Prelude engine, although similar in displacement to its predecessor, is quite different in proportion. Rather than the 77 mm bore and 94 mm stroke of the 1751, the 1829 has a bore of 80 mm and a stroke of 91 mm. These relatively squat

dimensions reduced the height of the engine 2.5 in., allowing a lower hood. The compression ratio increased from 8.8:1 to 9.4:1. The internal changes boosted power greatly, from 75 hp at 4800 rpm and 96 lb-ft of torque at 3000 rpm in 1982 to 97 hp at 5500 rpm and 105 lb-ft of torque at 4000 rpm in 1984. Besides the reduced 0-60 mph time, the new car covered the quarter mile from a standing start in 17.2 seconds at 78.5 mph.

This engine was produced for the Accord as well beginning in 1984. In 1985, for all Preludes and most Accords, the engine displacement was increased to 1955 cc. The bore of the 1955 is greater at 82.7 mm, while the stroke is the same at 91 mm. In 1986 the 1955 engine gained fuel injection (fuel injection had also been offered in the 1985 Accord SEi whose engine displaced 1829 cc). The fuel-injected engines retained the two intake valves and single exhaust valve, but did away with the auxiliary valves and CVCC system. They used electronic port fuel injection, meaning that the fuel flow is controlled by a computer and that an individual fuel injector is pointed directly into the intake port shared by each pair of intake valves. Honda calls the system PGM-FI, meaning Programmed Fuel Injection. The fuel injection and greater displacement upped the power to 110 hp at 5500 rpm and 114 lb-ft of torque at 4500 rpm (101 hp at 5500 rpm and 108 lb-ft of torque at 2500 rpm for the Accord SEi).

Civic
Third generation, 1984-87

In 1984, Honda departed from Civic tradition; nearly all of the features that had brought success were rethought and surprisingly few retained. While the first two Civics had rounded, upright styling, the third-generation Civic was wedge-shaped, sharp-cornered and squat. And although performance had always been potential to be developed by specialty tuners, in the new car it was standard equipment—a selling point for the dealers. And, while the second-generation Civic's persona was torn between the Accord's aspirations for refinement and the original Civic's sports-commuter compromises, the third-generation cars pinpointed these problems with a range of versions customized for each need.

The two-seater Civic CRX, the most significant of these individual applications, established a Honda reputation for high performance and trendy style. The CRX 1500 was the first true sports car with front-wheel drive. And it had race-winning performance; it accelerated to 60 mph in 10.1 seconds, covered a quarter mile from rest in 17.6 seconds at 78.5 mph and produced 0.813 g of lateral acceleration on a skid pad. And when the CRX Si—a fuel-injected version of the CRX 1500—was introduced in 1985, those numbers improved to 8.7 seconds for a 0–60 mph run, 16.7 seconds at 82.5 mph in the quarter mile and 0.82 g on the skid pad.

The CRX 1300 had a completely different role to fill. With a smaller 1342 cc engine that included friction-reducing two-ring pistons, a number of lightweight components and special low-rolling-resistance tires, the CRX 1300 was 1984's US fuel-mileage champion with a rating of 51 mpg. This high-mileage tradition carried on from 1985 through 1987 as a special 1488 engine was developed for its successor, the CRX HF (the HF designation stood for high fuel efficiency). Specialized Civics were also offered for those with families or other needs for additional seating, such as a four-seater hatchback, four-door sedan and station wagon.

Despite the wide variation, each version shared most of its components with the others. An overriding philosophy developed by Honda, referred to as the M/M Concept which stood for maximum interior space/minimal exterior space, guided the engineers as they designed the third-generation Civic. This resulted in two major breaks with previous designs: the first new Civic engine since the CVCC of 1975, and all-new suspension, with torsion bars in front and a beam axle in back, also known as a straight axle.

As with previous Civics, the third generation is frameless; a unibody design allows the sheet-metal body parts to provide the strength of a conventional frame. However, the front suspension and steering rack are bolted to a subframe which in turn is bolted across the underside of the body. The third-generation Civic marked a return to radius rods to control the tendency of the uprights to move forward or backward under acceleration or braking. These radius rods are unlike any used before, though. In fact, if you took an A-arm off a traditional American car's front suspension and cut it in half, the back half would look about like one of the Civic's two radius rods. From behind the upright, one of these radius rods attaches to the subframe through a bushing. The rod runs straight forward about half its length and then bends outward at nearly a 90 degree angle. The forward end of the rod, which points practically sideways, holds a ball joint to which the upright is attached.

The top of the upright is bolted to a MacPherson strut that is like those in earlier Civics except that it is not surrounded by a coil spring. Instead, a lateral link, which is bolted to the front side of the radius rod near the ball joint, is connected to a torsion bar.

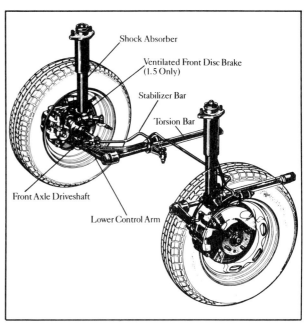

The third-generation Civic and the 1984–87 CRX share a torsion bar front suspension. The design allowed Honda to lower the front fenders and hood for a wedge-shaped profile.

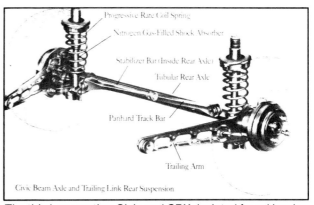

The third-generation Civic and CRX deviated from Honda practice in the rear as well as the front, by using a beam axle with trailing arms. Again, the layout was compact; it also allowed Honda to closely control the toe of the rear wheels as the suspension moved up and down. This produced more-predictable handling.

The inner end of the lateral link pivots in a bushing and has a splined female hub into which the front end of the torsion bar, with its male spline, mates. The rear end of the torsion bar is fixed so that it will not rotate. The torsion bar is located in a torque tube in which it may twist as the suspension rises and falls. The torque tube is bolted to the subframe so that the torsion bar is held in line with the length of the car. The front suspension is topped off with an anti-roll bar mounted behind the axis of the front wheels. The center of the anti-roll bar bolts to the subframe through a pair of clamps and bushings, and its ends attach to the radius rods through a long bolt and a set of bushings, called anti-roll bar links.

The rear suspension was non-independent for the first time. The third-generation Civic uses a tubular beam axle that stretches between and just behind the rear wheels, and to which several locating arms are attached. Reaching forward from each end of the axle tube are a pair of brackets. Attached to the left-side bracket are a stub axle, a trailing arm and a brake backing plate. The wheel hub, brake drum and wheel are attached to the hub which contains the rear wheel bearings. The trailing arm is stamped steel and runs forward to a mounting to which it attaches with a bushing and cross bolt. The right side is similar but more complicated. Instead of the stub axle being bolted directly to the axle-tube bracket, they are attached through a bearing that allows the trailing arm and brake assembly to rotate on the bracket. Resisting this rotation, however, is a linkage connected on one end to the trailing arm and on the other to a torsion bar mounted inside the axle tube. This torsion bar is the rear anti-roll bar and is attached to the suspension just on the right side. This is sufficient for the bar to resist roll to the right or left, though.

Other attachments to the rear axle include a Panhard rod and the shock absorbers. The Panhard rod looks like a lateral link used in independent suspensions except that it is much longer. It attaches to the front of the axle tube on the right side and to the bottom of the car on the left side; it resists side-to-side movement of the axle. The shock absorbers attach to brackets on the front side of the axle tube. They look like struts because they have sleeves on them to support the bottom of the rear coil springs; the tops of the springs are supported by cups in the fender wells. Since these large shock absorbers do not dictate the path traveled by the suspension, they are not termed struts.

Honda deviated from its previous independent rear suspensions for two reasons. First, the beam axle reduced camber and toe change as the suspension moved up and down—minimal change is vital for stability when cornering or braking hard, and over bumps. Second, although there is a lot of hardware involved in the beam axle, its trailing arms and Panhard rod, the suspension is compact. It steals little space from the passenger or luggage compartments.

Similarly making use of the M/M Concept is the front suspension's design. By using torsion bars under the car rather than coil springs in the fender wells, and by keeping all suspension components behind the engine, Honda was able to lower the cowl, fenders and hood dramatically. This improved appearance, aerodynamics and forward visibility. And overall, the size and weight of the new CRXs and Civics fell in line with their predecessors. The 1984 CRX measures 144.7 in. long, the 1984 Civic

In designing the 1984 CRX, as well as the Civics, Honda engineers followed what they called the M/M Concept, meaning maximum interior space/minimal exterior space. That required a complete redesign of the car, from engines to suspension. The basic platform was used for the CRX, the various Civics and the Acura Integra.

150 in. and the 1983 Civic 148.4 in. The 1984 CRX 1300 weighs 1,713 lb., the Civic 1500, 1,863 lb. and the 1983 Civic 1500, 1,867 lb.

Both the front and rear suspensions from the third-generation are used by the Acura Integra, introduced in the United States in 1987. It is related to the Civic like the second-generation Civic is to the first Prelude. The 1984–87 CRXs and Civics share platforms with the Integra as well as between themselves. These systems are the same basic designs, although many of the components will not interchange because of detail differences.

Like the suspension systems, the engines were completely new, although certain features harked back to the first 1170 Civic engine. For instance, the block and cylinder head were both aluminum. The block shares the open-deck design over the 1200 engines. And the cylinders are siamesed, although in this case the cylinders are cast in a single group of four, with no water jacket between any of the cylinders, rather than in pairs as on the 1200. Siamesed cylinders allow a more compact engine block.

This new engine series was produced in two displacements: 1342 and 1488 cc. The former has a bore of 74 mm and stroke of 78 mm. The latter uses the traditional 1488 dimensions with a bore of 74 mm and stroke of 86.5 mm.

The 1342 engine was produced in 1984 for the CRX 1300, and in 1984 and 1985 for the Civic 1300. It is a carbureted CVCC engine with a main intake valve, an auxiliary intake valve and an exhaust valve. As mentioned, this engine is a low-friction design with just one compression ring and one oil control ring per piston. Its role was high fuel mileage, a goal helped by the high 10.0:1 compression ratio. In 1985, the displacement for this special low-friction engine was upped to 1488 cc; otherwise, it retained the features of the 1342.

The twelve-valve 1488 is the component most responsible for Honda's newfound performance image. This engine, used in all but the high-mileage cars, added a second main intake valve to the cylinder head, increasing high-rpm engine breathing which in turn raised the engine's power. While Honda called this a twelve-valve cylinder head, there were actually sixteen valves in the carbureted version—the additional four being auxiliary valves for the CVCC system.

In 1985, Honda offered a fuel-injected 1488 in the CRX for the first time. As it did with the Accord SEi the same year, Honda eliminated the engine's CVCC system when it added fuel injection. Output jumped from 76 hp at 6000 rpm and 84 lb-ft of torque at 3500 rpm for the carbureted twelve-valve to 91 hp at 5500 rpm and 93 lb-ft of torque at 4500 rpm for the fuel-injected twelve-valve. This engine was offered from 1985 through 1987 in the CRX Si, and in 1986 and 1987 in the Civic Si.

The first-generation Integra made its debut in 1986 with power-assisted steering, four-wheel disc brakes and a responsive fuel-injected 1.6 liter, sixteen-valve double-overhead-camshaft engine. The car was available in both three-door and five-door versions.

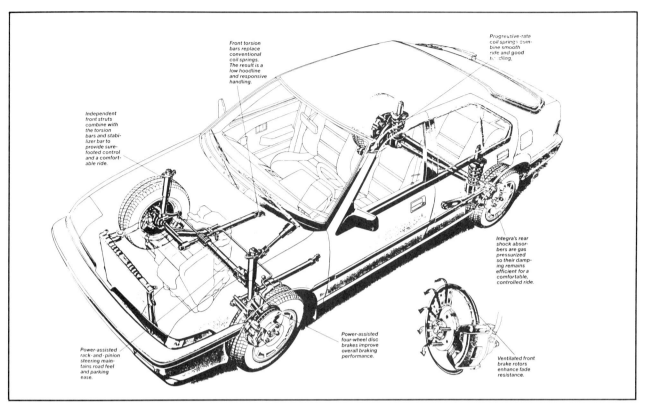

The 1987–89 Acura Integra used the third-generation Civic's basic chassis and suspension layout, but added four-wheel disc brakes.

The engines in the third-generation cars broke from Civic tradition in other ways. For the first time, the toothed camshaft drive belt drove the water pump as well as the cam. And while the oil pump had previously been located in the oil sump and driven by a long shaft geared to the middle of the camshaft, in the third-generation cars the oil pump is located at the front of the engine. Its rotor and housing slip over the nose of the crankshaft and the rotor is keyed to the crankshaft. The distributor is still driven by the camshaft, but directly off its end rather than through gears.

On carbureted models, a mechanical fuel pump drives off a lobe near the end of the camshaft. On fuel-injected models, an electric fuel pump is located near the gas tank. At the bottom end of the engine, the aluminum main-bearing girdle returned, looking similar to that on the Civic 1200 but lacking mounts and oil passages for the oil pump, no longer needed because of its new location.

Unavailable in the United States in the third-generation cars was a related high-performance engine displacing 1590 cc. This was the top option in Japanese and European market CRXs in 1986 and 1987, and was used in the Acura Integra as well. This engine has sixteen valves, double overhead camshafts, electronic port fuel injection, a bore of 75 mm and a stroke of 90 mm. Using the European rating system, the engine for the CRX 1.6i–16 produces 125 hp at 6500 rpm and 103 lb-ft of torque at 5500 rpm. The additional power allows the CRX 1.6i–16 to accelerate from 0 to 60 mph in 7.5 seconds and through the quarter mile at 16 seconds.

As with the preceding line of Civics, the third-generation cars were facelifted halfway through their life—in 1986. There was little change overall; the most apparent change was the addition of aerodynamic headlights that replaced the previous rectangular units.

Accord
Third generation, 1986–1989

Softer, smoother, slicker. These goals, combined with styling that makes the third-generation Accord look much like a hatchback or four-door Prelude, sum up the changes generally. Specifically, comparing four-door versions (1986 Accord LXi versus 1985 Accord SEi), the third-generation car is longer (178.5 versus 175.4 in.), lower (53.3 versus 54.1 in.) and wider (66.7 versus 65 in.). It is also much heavier (2,810 versus 2,440 lb.), a bit more powerful (110 hp at 5500 rpm from the 1955 cc twelve-valve engine versus 101 hp at 5800 rpm from the 1829 cc twelve-valve) and much more aerodynamic (comparing hatchbacks, a coefficient of drag of 0.31 versus 0.41).

The better aerodynamics and enlarged engine combined to produce nearly equal acceleration from the heavier 1986 Accord, compared to the 1985 version. They achieved 0–60 mph in identical times of 9.8 seconds, and the quarter mile in identical times of 17.3 seconds at practically the same speeds (79 versus 79.5 mph).

The third-generation Accord adopted the double wishbone front suspension of the Prelude and was the first Honda to use the same basic layout for the rear suspension as well. The other improvement in handling and ride came from a lengthened wheelbase. The distance between the front and rear wheels for the 1986 Accord four-door is 102.4 versus 96.5 in. for the previous version.

Integra
First generation, 1987–89

In essence, the Acura Integra is a rebodied third-generation Civic with the double-overhead-camshaft engine from the CRX 1.6i–16. In many ways, though, the Integra is much more. It is one of the two models that launched Honda's upscale Acura division through a new network of dealers. While the Integra became the entry-level Acura, it had to be refined enough, powerful enough and composed enough when driven hard to be a viable option for customers who previously had shopped only the European makes. As always, Honda accomplished these tough goals through refinement and attention to detail. It was not enough to have a Euro-contender on paper; the Integra had to look and feel the part as well.

Honda did this by taking components from one of the best-handling front-wheel-drive platforms on the market—that of the Civic/CRX series—and adapting them to the Integra's new body. So, the torsion bar front suspension and beam axle rear suspension used so successfully in the third-generation Civic and CRX found a new home on the Integra.

The powerplant was important for selling the Integra to a new group of customers, and the 1590 cc sixteen-valve engine is one of Honda's best. As introduced in the United States, it produced 113 hp at 6250 rpm, and 99 lb-ft of torque at 5500 rpm. The engine accelerates 0–60 mph in 9.3 seconds, and through the quarter mile in 17 seconds at 80 mph.

The Integra was introduced as a hatchback with three or five doors. The three-door is 168.5 in. long while the five-door is 171.3 in. long. Both are 65.6 in. wide and 53 in. tall. The three-door weighs 2,325 lb. while the five-door weighs 2,475 lb.

Prelude
Third generation, 1988–

Again, with the introduction of the third Prelude, a major goal was refinement. In this case, the appearance of the car changed little. A slight rearranging of the sheet metal appeared to be the extent of the change, but in fact the car had been redesigned from top to bottom. While most of this re-engineering was aimed at making an existing concept better, innovation was also part of the formula: On the 1988 Prelude, Honda introduced four-wheel steering.

The idea of steering the rear wheels in the opposite direction from the front wheels to gain maneuverability for parking has been discussed and experimented with for decades. But the 1988 Prelude was the first car that also steered the rear wheels in the same direction as the front wheels to enhance stability in turns and to provide a surer response to the initial turning of the steering wheel.

The third-generation Prelude can be found with conventional two-wheel steering as well. In this iteration, it has a double wishbone front suspension as did its predecessor, and it uses the same basic layout in the rear as the third-generation Accord does. Several extra components are used by Honda in its all-mechanical, four-wheel steering system

First, the steering rack has an extra pinion gear that is driven by the rack. Attached to this gear is an output shaft that runs rearward to another steering gear at the center of the rear suspension. The gears and an eccentric shaft inside the gearbox are arranged so that small movements of the steering wheel to the left or right turn the rear wheels left or right up to 1.5

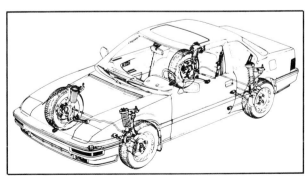

The 1988 Prelude, introduced in mid 1987, was the first Honda to use the company's double wishbone suspension front and rear.

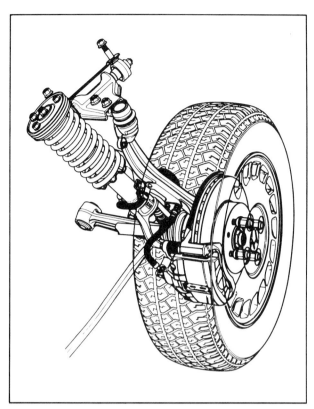

The third-generation Prelude retained the previous model's double wishbone suspension in the front and adapted a version of it in the rear as well—a Honda first.

degrees. Once the steering wheel is turned more than 140 degrees, the rear wheels begin to return to the straight-ahead position. When the steering wheel is turned more than 246 degrees left or right, as it would be in a tight turn, the rear wheels steer the opposite direction—right or left—up to 5.3 degrees. The motion from the rear steering gear is transferred to the rear uprights through tie rods.

On the test track, the difference between the two-wheel-steer and four-wheel-steer cars is difficult to feel or measure, with one exception: In very tight turns such as a first-gear hairpin, the four-wheel-steer Prelude feels as though it's hinged in the middle. In normal turns, a difference is hard to identify. To some, turning is a bit more stable with four wheel steering, to others it just feels a little numb. Still, this is a system that Honda and others will be refining and further improvements are expected.

Other, more subtle changes can be found on the third-generation Prelude. Like the third-generation Accord, the third-generation Prelude is longer, wider and heavier than its predecessor. Its length is 175.6 versus 168.9 in., its width is 67.3 versus 66.5 in., and its weight is 2,705 versus 2,180 lb. To

improve upon performance, the engine had to be reworked. The displacement was increased 3 cc— from 1955 cc to 1958 cc, with a new bore and stroke of 81 and 95 mm—and the engine was redesigned.

Two versions were offered: a carbureted twelve-valve (104 hp with manual transmission, 105 hp with automatic) and a sixteen-valve double-overhead-camshaft version with electronic port fuel injection that produces 135 hp at 6200 rpm and 127 lb-ft of torque at 4500 rpm. Both engines are all-aluminum. They are slanted more than their predecessors (18 degrees rather than 15 degrees), and they are slanted in the opposite direction (toward the firewall) to allow a lower hood. The sixteen-valve engine uses a dual-stage intake manifold with one tract for low-rpm use and an additional, larger tract for high-rpm use that is controlled by a vacuum-actuated valve. The second tract opens at 5000 rpm. This engine propels the Prelude 0–60 mph in 9.3 seconds and through the quarter mile in 16.8 seconds at 83.5 mph.

Civic
Fourth generation, 1988–

The 1988 CRXs and Civics were what the 1980 Civic was to its predecessor—a thorough refinement of a successful concept. The cars' styling is the clearest key to this. From any direction the silhouettes of the fourth-generation CRXs, and particularly the Civics, are similar to their predecessors, except that their corners are rounder, the edges are softer and the windshields lie at steeper angles. This melted-butter look serves two purposes. First, it is up to date: the soft aerodynamic look is the current style. Second, it truly improves the aerodynamics, increasing speed and fuel economy. The only penalties are small increases in overall size and weight. For instance, a 1987 CRX Si is 144.8 in. long, 63.9 in. wide and weighs 1,890 lb. A 1988 CRX Si is longer at 147.8 in., wider at 65.7 in. and weighs more at 2,017 lb.

Even so, Honda continued to make good use of the M/M Concept for maximizing the interior space while taking up a minimal amount of room on the road. Its application in the fourth-generation cars is more sophisticated, however. As in 1984, this is prevalent mechanically in the front and rear suspensions, and the engines.

Honda's double wishbone design is used front and rear. The front suspension follows the design laid out for the second-generation Prelude. The rear suspension, however, is updated from the Prelude and Accord. It is dominated by a pair of beefy, stamped-steel trailing arms that are attached through a bushing and short shaft bolted across the underside

The 1988 and later CRXs kept general proportions of the original model, while updating the car's appearance with rounded corners, a reduced rear-hatch angle and an overall aerodynamic updating.

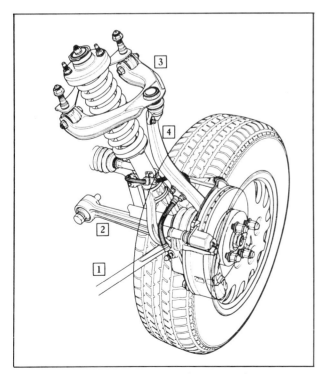

In 1988, the fourth-generation Civic and CRX adopted Honda's double wishbone front suspension.

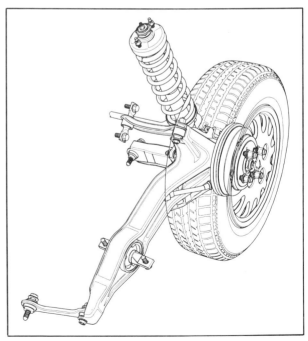

In the rear, the fourth Civic and CRX used a new version of the double wishbone rear suspension with a new toe-control link to keep the rear wheels in line as the suspension moves up and down.

of the unibody. The rear end of the trailing arm forms the upright. Attached to it through bushings and cross bolts are a pair of lateral links, one on the top and one on the bottom. The trailing arm has one other unusual feature: Rather than ending at its front bushings, it extends forward several inches and attaches through bushings and cross bolts to a third lateral link. This extra piece is called a toe-control link and solves one of the problems that the third-generation Civic's solid axle was chosen for—to limit toe change under cornering and braking, and over bumps. By using this multi-link design, Honda achieves the stability of the beam axle, and retains the rough-road capabilities and light weight of an independent suspension. A U-shaped anti-roll bar trails behind the lower lateral links to which it is attached through short vertical links.

The repackaging of the fourth-generation Civic engines is equally impressive. The block is similar to that of the third-generation, although iron caps are used in the main-bearing girdle and the displacements are different. The engines for all except the CRX Si and four-wheel-drive station wagon displace 1493 cc, and have a bore of 75 mm and stroke of 84.5 mm. The CRX Si and four-wheel-drive wagon engines displace 1590 cc, and like the earlier 1590 from the CRX 1.6i–16 and the Acura Integra, have a bore of 75 mm and stroke of 90 mm.

All the fourth-generation engines are fuel injected, have non-CVCC combustion chambers and sixteen-valve cylinder heads, except the CRX HF engine which uses an eight-valve head. But rather than adopting the double overhead camshafts as on the earlier 1590, the Civic sixteen-valve uses a single overhead camshaft with sixteen narrow cam lobes and rocker arms. The extra weight of the rocker arms (the cams act directly on the valves in the Acura head) lowers the upper rpm limit, but greatly reduces the size of the cylinder head. This allows the hoodlines of the fourth-generation cars to be lower than the already trim lines of the previous CRXs and Civics.

The Si and HF engines are port fuel injected, using Honda's electronic system. The standard 1493 engine uses a different version of this system with just two injectors located at the opening of the intake manifold to the throttle. The Si engine produces 105 hp at 6000 rpm and 98 lb-ft of torque at 5000 rpm. The sixteen-valve 1493 produces 92 hp at 6000 rpm and 89 lb-ft of torque at 4500 rpm in all models except the base Civic hatchback, in which it produces 70 hp at 5500 rpm and 83 lb-ft of torque at 3000 rpm. The eight-valve CRX HF engine produces 62 hp at 4500 rpm and 90 lb-ft of torque at 2000 rpm.

The new CRX Si lives up to its high-performance reputation. It will accelerate to 60 mph in 8.2 seconds, and will cover the quarter mile from rest in 16.4 seconds at 84 mph. However, its lateral acceleration on a skid pad, as measured by *Road & Track* magazine, is lower at 0.78 g than that for the previous CRX. Nonetheless, on the racetrack, the new CRX has proved significantly faster than the old, and is a better balanced and more sophisticated car overall.

3

Making a game plan

The rules of thumb for improving a car are much like those used by reporters to write news articles. Their reports must answer these basic questions: who, what, where, when, why and how? Approaching car modifications in the same manner can save headaches and disappointment. An auto hop-up project that fails to deliver the expected performance can be disheartening. So, like a news reporter, investigate and dig out the basic facts before proceeding.

When applying the journalistic "five Ws and one H" to a car project, start with this general question, *Why* are you dissatisfied with the car as it stands, and *what* do you hope to accomplish by modifying it? Is its acceleration too weak; are you looking for a bit more snap or are you searching for the punch of a racing engine? Is its handling too sloppy; do you want to tighten up the ride a little or do you want it to drive like an all-out sports car? Is the car's appearance

Decide what to do with your Honda before thinking about what to do to it. This 1988 Civic Si, undergoing track testing for *Grassroots Motorsports* magazine, has a single modification: a set of racing-style, high-performance street tires. The B. F. Goodrich Comp T/A R–1 tires are ideal for a stock-class autocrosser like this Civic Si.

This is also an essentially stock Honda—a 1988 CRX Si, one of a two-car team that won the SCCA's 1988 and 1989 Escort Endurance Championships. The Jackson Racing-prepared CRX—shown here winning the 1988 championship in the season finale at Sebring, Florida—has a single purpose: winning races. It never sees the street, even though it's street legal. It either is on the racetrack or in the shop for between-race refurbishing.

too bland; would a simple change like new wheels and tires help, or would you rather build a whole new image with an aero body kit? If you're not sure what you're looking for at the beginning of a project, you're likely to be disappointed once the work is done. And remember, Honda has balanced acceleration, performance and appearance of most of its models well. Whatever changes you make should be as close to factory quality as possible; the combination of several half-baked modifications can result in a car that's less satisfying than the factory-stock version.

Next on the list are these questions: *Who* will do the work? If it's you, *how* will you carry out the changes? If this sort of thing is new to you, start by adding simple accessories and work up to more complicated improvements. If it is a shop that will carry out your plans, does it have the expertise necessary; does it know Hondas; has it undertaken jobs like this before? Ask to see samples of its work.

If you are like many enthusiasts and trust the care of your car to no one else, *where* will you make your modifications? Working out on the driveway to install wheels and tires, anti-roll bars or an exhaust system is one thing. But delving into the insides of an engine or transaxle is quite another, requiring a room free from dirt and dust. Even a garage or workshop might not be suitable, if it is leaky or its

doors must be opened often while the component is disassembled.

Finally, *when* must the work be completed? Projects almost always take longer than planned—even something as simple as a wheel-and-tire swap. For involved work, many enthusiasts will double their time estimates, or even triple them. Examples of time-wasters include wheel-and-tire combinations that rub fender lips or suspension components, throttle linkages on non-stock carburetors that must be homemade or modified to work, and internal engine components that must be hand-fitted. This applies to many bolt-on products as well as special racing parts.

Despite these pitfalls, car projects can be rewarding, and substantial improvements in performance and appearance can be obtained. When Honda or any other major manufacturer designs and outfits a model, it compromises many features to make the car suitable for thousands of customers. So it's natural that the car is not tailored to your specifications. If you are particular about driving, the car needs to be fine-tuned to your needs. In fact, tuners is the term used in Europe for mechanics who hop up cars and make special parts for them. There the modification of small sports cars and sports sedans has gone on for decades.

Form follows function

Of all the questions to ask yourself, the most important is, What do you hope to accomplish? Car tuning can be subtle or radical, with the wildest modifications resulting in a car suited only for racing or show. Striking the right balance is the key. So take some time to map out your goals and make sure the equipment you choose is likely to deliver the results you're looking for.

Many improvements—changing tires, wheels, struts, anti-roll bars, springs, exhaust or air filters, or adding gauges, air dams or body kits—need not change the car's ability to serve as transportation—they just make it more fun. The widest selection of parts is sold with this in mind.

Some drivers modify their cars for competition reasons. They want the car to go faster, stop quicker and corner harder to win races. Since many Hondas carry the moniker sports sedan or sports coupe, they are entered in sports car events like road races and autocrosses. The Sports Car Club of America (SCCA) is the largest group sanctioning these events. The SCCA, and other clubs like it, offers categories of classes so that cars with equal modifications compete against one another. Further, within

The author's Civic 1200 splits the difference, being used for daily transportation, and competing as a Street Prepared entry in autocrosses and as an Improved Touring car on high-speed tracks. The carburetors are alternated between a pair of sidedraft Dell'Ortos or a downdraft Weber, depending on whether the car is being used in Street Prepared or Improved Touring. No other changes are made and both carburetion set-ups are used on the street.

each category, they set out classes so that similar cars run against one another.

A road race is much as its name implies, a race on a track that twists and turns like a country road. A typical road racing track is two miles long with a dozen left- and right-hand turns, and a straightaway. An autocross is a time trial in which only one car runs on the course at a time. Each driver gets three runs from a standing start. Each driver's single best time is compared with his or her competitors'; the lowest time in each class wins. A typical autocross course is a half-mile long, mapped out on a parking lot or air strip with orange traffic cones called pylons.

Racing theory trickles down to the streets

Learning about the classifications for these events is interesting because Hondas make excellent competition cars, and have won a number of state, regional and national championships. Moreover, it's valuable because the cars' improvements often can be applied to Hondas that will never see competition.

Many of the rules are based on changes commonly made to improve performance. Another way to look at it is that if you keep your changes within the rules, you can try an autocross and see if competi-

Jinx Jordan of Vernon, Connecticut, uses a third-generation Civic in SCCA Street Prepared autocrossing. The D Street Prepared national champion in 1987 and 1988 in a CRX 1300, Jordan built this Civic 1500 in 1989 to compete in Pro Solo, in which D Street Prepared cars, like the CRX 1300, are combined with cars from C Street Prepared. According to Jordan and Chuck Noonan of CRE/Performance in Barre, Massachusetts, the smaller hatch opening of the Civic gives it more rigidity than the CRX and that the longer wheelbase makes its handling more predictable. These features make the Civic 1500 more desirable in C Street Prepared or Pro Solo's Street Prepared 3, they believe.

SCCA results show Bob Endicott's 1984 CRX with a CRX Si engine to be one of the fastest C Street Prepared Hondas in the country. Once Endicott of Long Beach, California, pulls off the magnetic numbers and sponsor decals, the CRX is deceptively stock-appearing.

On the other hand, the C Street Prepared CRX of Memphis, Tennessee's Grady Wood Jr. looks the part of a race car, with or without numbers and lettering. The difference is the aggressive body kit. The deep front air dam, wide fender flares and nose-down attitude mark Wood's CRX as a racer, even though it's mechanically similar to Endicott's CRX.

tion appeals to you. Because the rules must be strictly enforced, a seemingly innocuous improvement could bump your car up to a higher category, making it uncompetitive. For instance, a non-stock air filter would force you out of a Stock autocross class into a Street Prepared class where the competitors would have engines with unlimited carburetion, headers and non-stock exhaust systems, and many other modifications. Or a mild, non-stock camshaft—even though intended for street use—would bump you from a Stock or Street Prepared class all the way into a Race Prepared class in which hand-built, tube-framed cars with all-out racing engines compete. So if competition interests you in the least, check out your local club's rules before modifying your car.

Two categories of road racing classes bear discussion: Showroom Stock and Improved Touring. There are several other more advanced categories like GT, Sports Racer and Formula, but in them, the main Honda part considered usable is the engine. In GT, Honda body parts would be used, but nearly everything else is handmade for racing.

Showroom Stock requires cars to run almost exactly as delivered on the dealer's showroom floor and be no more than four years old. A few safety equipment additions are required, and among them are a roll cage, fire extinguisher, racing-type seatbelt harness and a window net to keep the driver's arms within the car in case of an accident. Otherwise, no changes may be made. Even adjustments like ignition timing must meet factory specifications. Showroom Stock cars can serve dual transportation-competition

purposes, but usually only as a second car. The lap-after-lap punishment a car takes on the track means that between-race maintenance can be extensive. Also, the roll cage can get in the way in day-to-day use. The better Showroom Stock teams are worth observing and learning from, however. They gain significant performance increases by disassembling parts—particularly the engine—and rebuilding them so that they meet factory specifications precisely. And they maintain their cars meticulously, not allowing wear to degrade performance.

Improved Touring is an outgrowth of Showroom Stock racing and is for cars more than four years old. The safety equipment requirements are the same, except that Improved Touring cars must also have the steering wheel lock removed. Unlike Showroom Stock, Improved Touring allows a number of modifications for improved performance. So this category offers the advantages of using an older car that the driver may already own or at least won't have to pay so much for, and it provides a chance to experiment with certain mechanical modifications to see what results in faster laps. Among the changes allowed are:

• A Weber carburetor on a stock manifold (certain cars are allowed this change; most Hondas are included).
• Any fuel pump.
• Air filter removal or replacement.
• Any ignition system.
• An exhaust header and custom exhaust system.
• Oil-system modifications like baffled oil pans,

When Chuck Noonan moved out of C Street Prepared and into E Prepared after winning three national SCCA autocrossing championships in a CRX 1500, he did it with this Civic 1500. Besides the body and wheelbase advantages shared with Jinx Jordan's visually similar Civic, the rules allow Civics to use power steering in the Prepared Category whereas CRXs may not. The difference, with a limited slip differential and racing slicks, is enormous, Noonan says. The power steering overcomes the vicious torque steer that such a combination produces.

an oil cooler, or an oil accumulator like an Accusump which stores oil and, through air pressure, injects it into the engine's oiling system whenever pressure drops.

- Any clutch.
- Final-drive gears of any ratio that can be installed in the transaxle without modification.
- Any shock absorbers that mount in the original position, and any struts or strut inserts.
- Any suspension springs that will fit in the original position.
- Any anti-roll bars, traction bars, Panhard rods or Watts linkages.
- Camber and caster adjustment plates for strut towers.
- Any suspension bushings, including eccentric (offset) bushings for suspension adjustment.
- Any brake pads, linings, hoses or fluid.
- Ventilated brake backing plates may be modified for ventilation and brake ducts.
- Pressure-limiting brake proportioning valves to adjust the amount of brake pressure going to the front or rear.
- Wider wheels—the exact sizes are listed class by class—and any tire approved by the Department of Transportation. Also, rolled-under fender lips, but no flares, and tires must fit under the fenders.
- Air dams.

- Driver's seat, but not the passenger's seat.
- Steering wheel, as long as the new one is not wooden.
- Gauges.
- Rear seat removal.
- Limited-slip or locked differential.

While these road racing rules make a good list of changes from which to choose, examining common autocrossing rules—in this case, the SCCA's—may be even more valuable because many autocrossing classes are designed for cars that will be driven to the event and then back home after the competition. For that reason, we'll concentrate on the Stock and Street Prepared categories which were drawn up with street use in mind. Autocrossing's Stock classes are much like road racing's Showroom Stock, but more liberal— more modifications are allowed. Some of these modifications are:

- Any steering wheel, although the new one may be no more than one inch smaller or larger in diameter.
- A roll bar or cage.
- Different tire sizes.
- Any wheels of the same diameter and of a width within 0.25 in. of stock.
- Shock absorbers or struts as long as they attach to the car in the stock manner.
- Front anti-roll bars.

Angelo D. Roberson of Birmingham, Alabama, autocrosses a race-prepared Civic 1200 in D Prepared. The interior is gutted of stock trim, a full roll cage is fitted as are a number of handmade suspension parts and the engine is tuned for racing only.

• Exhaust system, behind the catalytic converter (or manifold if there is no converter) as long as it meets the standards of the state in which the car is registered.

Street Prepared allows a wide variety of modifications, in short, just about anything except a racing engine or chassis, or racing slicks (even then, the fastest Street Prepared cars use tires that are specially made for competition and are street-legal as well). In fact, a few Street Prepared changes can render a car unusable for routine transportation, particularly in states with strict emissions laws. But many of these cars strike a good balance between competition and street use. Here's a listing of the major modifications allowed (the Stock category changes are permitted as well):

• Any oil pan, coolers or accumulators, although the engine's oiling system must remain stock.

• Any ignition system.

• Any carburetors, fuel injection, intake manifolds, fuel pumps or filters.

• Unrestricted exhaust headers and systems as long as they are quiet and exit behind the driver.

• Any flywheel or torque converter that attaches in the standard way, or any clutch.

• Suspension springs that attach in the stock manner.

• Suspension bushings as long as the new ones are not made from metal. Eccentric bushings are allowed. Bump stops may be changed or removed.

• Camber and caster adjustment plates on strut towers.

• Strut bars that are bolted between upper suspension mounting points or lower mounting points, but they may not be tied together or to other parts of the car.

• Front and rear anti-roll bars.

• A limited-slip differential, but not a locked differential. Stock-ratio final-drive gears are required.

• Any fully upholstered seat.

• Any steering wheel.

Mix and match

Although the rules vary between road racing's Improved Touring classes and autocrossing's Street Prepared classes, the two categories allow one other way to modify cars: updating and backdating. This allows you to choose the best components from different versions or years of a certain model—say, a CRX—and is particularly advantageous with Hon-

Construction of the tube-frame CRX built by King Motorsports of Milwaukee, Wisconsin, in 1988. Draped over the tube-frame chassis was a fiberglass replica CRX body. The engine was a 1.6 liter single-overhead-cam Mugen unit, which pumped out 210 horsepower. The result was a lightweight Honda with power to boot. The car won the SCCA GT3 class in 1989. *G. William Krause*

das. Often, by mixing and matching parts, you can produce a better performance combination than the factory. A transaxle from an earlier or later year, for instance, might have more useful gear ratios. The Si transaxles in particular often have lower final-drive ratios. The lower the gear ratio, the greater the acceleration. Keep in mind that the higher the number, the lower the gear reduction. For example, the 4.428:1 final-drive gear ratio of the 1986 CRX Si is lower than the 4.266:1 final-drive ratio of the standard 1986 CRX. There is a trade-off: A lower final-drive ratio will reduce fuel mileage and increase engine noise and wear somewhat. But such losses can prove worthwhile if the gain in performance is sufficient and the overall balance is not grossly changed. For competition purposes, the limits of parts swap-

King Motorsports' Mugen CRX as raced in the 1989 SCCA GT3 championship and driven by Jim Dentici. The engine is built up using Mugen parts and the effect is awesome.

Note the bodywork and wide wheel arches to cover the car's wheels. *King Motorsports*

King Motorsports' tube-frame CRX GT3 racer used double A-arm front suspension with its front-wheel-drive configuration—far from stock! *G. William Krause*

The office of the tube-frame CRX was pure race. The interior roll cage is part of the tube-frame chassis, the ultimate in rigidity and light weight. Firewall and dashboard are aluminum sheets. *G. William Krause*

King Motorsports of Milwaukee, Wisconsin, also built a tube-frame Integra, which it raced for several seasons. The tube-frame chassis was covered by a fiberglass Integra replica body, and the double-overhead-cam engine produced 210 horsepower. The car was sold by King to a race team based in California, which took second place in the 1989 SCCA GT3 championship. First place went to King's CRX. *G. William Krause*

ping like this are strictly spelled out; consult the latest rules before proceeding.

For street cars, the best guide is to stay within the same model and generation, or same engine family when picking and choosing parts. For instance, stay within the third-generation Civic and CRX line when looking at transaxles. Or keep to the CVCC engine line for cars so equipped. This way most parts will bolt directly into place without conversion.

There are two common and rewarding engine swaps within this vein. The first is installing a 1985-87 CRX Si engine in a standard, carbureted 1984-87 CRX, or putting the Si's non-CVCC cylinder head on the standard block. The first advantage is the fuel-injected engine's power—91 hp at 5500 rpm versus 76 hp at 6000 rpm. Installing the wiring harness and computer for the PGM-FI fuel-injection system in a carbureted car is difficult. Many bypass this by using a pair of Mikuni or Weber sidedraft carburetors which produce equivalent power.

King Motorsports' tube-frame Integra used a suspension set-up that was far from stock. With the engine removed, the tube framing and suspension are clearly seen in this photo. The front suspension relied on lower A-arms with offset springs and shocks. The rear end used a solid axle. *G. William Krause*

A Honda CRX ice racer with Jackson Racing parts and support. Ice racing is immensely popular in the Midwest during the long winters where racetracks are laid out by shoveling courses on frozen lakes with the snowbanks as the only boundaries. On the ice, front-wheel-drive cars lord over rear-wheel-drive cars to the point where two classes are needed to separate the two and give rear-drivers a chance. Hondas have consistently been among the top placers in the Production class. Note the spiked tires that provide at least some traction. *Tim Parker*

The Civic CVCC that ruled the Modified ice racing class in 1988–89. The car was built by OHV Motors, Eden Prairie, Minnesota, and featured a 1200 cc engine with nitrous oxide injection via dual Weber sidedraft carburetors. The chassis was semi-tube-frame and the rear wing over the rear window provided downforce. The removable hood rests on the roof. *Tim Parker*

The 1751 CVCC engine can be identified, when disassembled, by the spacing between cylinders. The 1751 cylinders are evenly spaced.

The 1488 and 1597 CVCC engines have a wide space between the two center cylinders.

The second advantage of using the Si engine in the base CRX 1500 is that the car has no sunroof and thus the body is lighter. This can be confirmed through the general specifications in this chapter. For instance, a 1985 CRX 1500 weighs 1,819 lb. while a CRX Si of the same year is sixty-four pounds heavier at 1,883 lb. Those looking for the greatest advantage choose the 1984 CRX which weighs 1,803 lb. It is three percent lighter than the 1987 CRX Si, which is the heaviest of the CRXs in the third-generation Civic family.

That 175 lb. difference is substantial in a lightweight car like a CRX. It's the equivalent of carrying a good-sized passenger all the time. Use of a CRX 1300 body would provide a greater weight saving, but because of certain competition rules, the CRX 1500 is the most common platform for this sort of swap. So if you're shopping for a Honda, check the specification charts and consider the weights of the different years and versions before making a choice.

The second engine swap frequently made is installing a 1751 CVCC engine from a 1979 Accord in a first-generation Civic CVCC or first-generation Accord 1600. The difference in power, particularly for the Civic, is substantial. The later 1751s are not usable in the earlier cars because of differences in crankshaft and flywheel flanges. But with no modifications other than the engine swap, a 1975 Civic CVCC can be increased from 53 hp at 5000 rpm to 72 hp at 4500 rpm.

Oscar Jackson, founder of Jackson Racing in Huntington Beach, California, likes to take the swap one step further. All 1751s in 1979, and 1751s with manual transaxles in 1980 had just two exhaust ports; they were siamesed. Cylinders 1 and 2, and 3

By using the extra space in the middle of the engine, Honda made the 1751 the same length as the earlier CVCC engines; it has the same mountings and appears identical from the outside.

The 1488 cylinder head shown here is a Canadian version without CVCC porting. These heads are sold by tuners as high-power replacements for CVCC cylinder heads. A spark plug hole takes up the spot normally used for the CVCC pre-chamber.

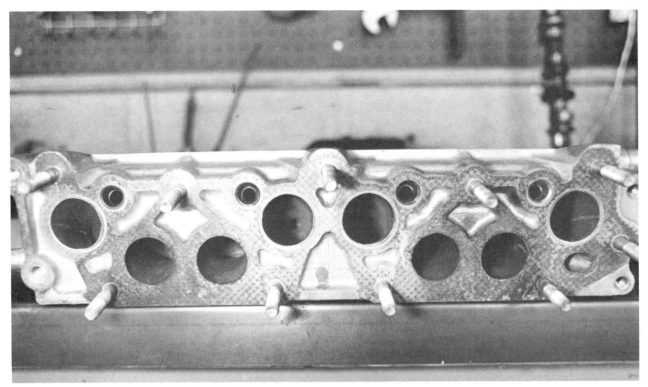

The CVCC cylinder head can be identified from the manifold surface by its CVCC ports along the upper face of the head.

The Canadian head is similar to the CVCC head but has no CVCC ports.

and 4 shared ports, to the detriment of exhaust flow and power output. However, 1751s in 1980 with automatic transaxles, and all 1751s in 1981 had cylinder heads with four exhaust ports. This better cylinder head will fit the 1979 block. The 1751s in 1982 and 1983, which also had separate exhaust ports, will not fit the early block.

Jackson describes this favorite combination of his, and the fine-tuning that rounds it out: "I have a lot of people who have even as late as '79 Civic CVCCs that are tired, worn out. They want more power, but they don't want to put a Weber carburetor on it because it gets them in trouble with the emission-control people." Because it is externally the same as the 1488 and 1597 CVCC engines, the emission controls can be retained, Jackson says. "You can use the original carburetor and intake manifold if you want to because it all bolts on that same motor. The exhaust manifold, instead of a two-bolt, is a three-bolt, but you get a three-bolt headpipe off an early Prelude and it bolts right up to the stock exhaust system. Suddenly you have a car that's absolutely stock under the hood. Especially in California

where we have visual underhood inspections, if one emissions control item is modified or missing, the car's illegal—no matter what comes out the tailpipe. Visually, if anything's missing, it's illegal. So, you see, a lot of what I tell you comes from living in California. And it's going to affect the rest of the country eventually."

In preparation for the swap, Jackson advises customers to start with a sound engine or short block like "these factory-rebuilt twelve-month, 12,000 mile guarantee motors; or the twelve-month, 12,000 mile bottom end (engine without cylinder head), get a four-port head, cut 0.040 inch off the head, get in there, do a little clean-up port work, put one of our headers on, or just leave the stock exhaust manifold on. Even with the stock exhaust manifold on, bolt the thing together, crank the distributor up—get it recurved so it has some advance to it because that's the one thing Hondas usually lack is any kind of advance curve—and zingo, you've got a car that humps and bumps. It doesn't make any noise, it idles like a kitten, gets 40 miles per gallon. That's a win all the way around. Let's say that car started at 60 hp and

The Civic and CRX line owe much to the Austin Mini in basic front-wheel-drive layout and two-box body configuration. In this case, the Mini of Valdosta, Georgia's Harold Knobel owes much to Honda as well. It's fitted with a CRX Si engine and transaxle. Knobel, a past SCCA national champion, autocrosses the car in D Modified and enters it in high-speed events as well.

you get 20 hp more, that's more than 30 percent. Suddenly 20 hp makes a big difference—a thirty-percent jump. And in a car as light as a Civic—those are 1,600 to 1,800 pound cars, depending on which one you bought—it makes sense to do that and you're not bastardizing the car. It's a good combination. You use the original linkage, you use the original exhaust system, the original transmission, mounts, shifter—everything original."

While purchasing the Accord engine together with its transaxle might seem reasonable, Jackson recommends against it, noting that the Civic used lower gear ratios that help acceleration. Refer to the specifications if this sort of mixing and matching interests you, and tailor the components to your needs.

Several engine swaps can benefit the Civic 1200 as well, particularly the 1973–77 versions. The first-generation Civic was imported to the United States with three versions of the basic 1200 engine. The first, in 1973 only, was the 1170 cc model EB1. The second, from 1974 through 1977, was the 1237 cc model EB2. The only difference between these two engines, other than year-to-year variations in tuning

for emissions control, were the cylinder-bore and piston diameters. The EB1 has 70 mm cylinders while the EB2 has 72 mm cylinders, accounting for the displacement increase. In 1978, the EB3 was introduced. It retained the 1237 cc displacement, but used a cylinder head with larger valves, improved intake and exhaust ports, a deeper combustion chamber and domed pistons to match the new chamber's greater volume.

An EB3 head can be used on an EB2 block, but only if the EB3 pistons are installed as well; otherwise, the compression ratio would be too low. The EB3 produces 55 hp at 5000 rpm, while the EB2 produces 52 hp at 5000 rpm and the EB1 50 hp at 5000 rpm. Although the three to five horsepower difference is small, the EB3's better cylinder head allows greater increases in power when improvements in carburetion, exhaust or the valvetrain are made. So it is the choice for the Civic 1200.

One further swap can benefit the Civic 1237 engine without great complication, if the engine is being rebuilt. By installing the crankshaft, connecting rods and flywheel from a 1980–83 1335 cc Civic engine, you can create a 1335 with a cross-flow

The CRX Si engine that fits snugly into Harold Knobel's Austin Mini. Note the dual sidedraft Weber carburetors and the prodigious amount of aluminum sheeting that serves as heat shield protection.

Low-mileage Honda engines from Japanese junkyards are being imported to the United States. Engines such as this Civic 1335 engine with 45,000 kilometers (about 28,000 miles) can be bought from importers inexpensively. The Japanese version is uncluttered, not even hav-ing an automatic choke, while the original US version is tangled with emission controls. To keep the car legal, the carburetor, ignition, intake and exhaust manifolds, and emission controls from the US engine are transferred to the Japanese engine.

cylinder head. The production 1335s use a CVCC cylinder head that makes less power. The 1335 crankshaft has an 82 mm stroke versus the 76 mm of the 1237. The 1335 connecting rods are shorter to compensate for the difference. The 1335 flywheel is required because the 1335 crankshaft flange uses a dowel pin to locate the flywheel and the 1237 crank does not.

A new source of Honda engines is becoming common in some parts of the country, particularly near seaports. Companies have sprung up to import used engines and transaxles from Japan. Laws that encourage the purchase of new cars there have resulted in a glut of low-mileage cars (often in the 30,000 mile range) in Japanese junkyards. The

Once the valves are adjusted, the valve and timing covers are replaced.

Additionally, routine maintenance is performed on the Japanese replacement engine before it is installed. The timing belt is replaced while it is accessible. Although this belt can last as long as the engine in first- and second-generation Civics, age and oil leakage are its enemies. Whenever an older timing belt can be easily changed, doing so is good insurance.

The new engine is then hoisted into place. This work can be undertaken in a home garage or driveway, but takes several days of hard work and use of special tools such as this rented hydraulic hoist.

imported engines and transaxles can save money, but often there are subtle variations between them and the US versions—particularly in carburetion and emission controls—and sometimes the differences are great. Before buying, inspect the component closely for compatibility.

In the case of transaxles, use the gear ratios from the specification charts to compare with the importer's cross-reference books. Generally, these components are best suited for non-performance cars because of their different specifications, but occasionally you can turn up something like a Civic RS engine—the high-performance Civic 1200 engine from Japan with twin sidedraft carburetors that, despite its 1170 cc displacement, produces about 68 hp at 6000 rpm. It might be worth buying.

Finally, because Honda's Japanese market engine-model designations do not exactly match those for engines originally sold in the United States, they should not be considered for competition. Most rules require the use of US specification parts.

The mixing and matching of Honda parts can be done on many levels. The installation of a later, more powerful engine in an earlier car may make sense for one person. The use of an imported used engine might save money for someone else. Or updating or backdating may play no part in another's plans; bolting on a set of stronger anti-roll bars may be all it takes to meet his or her goals. However, if your goals inch upward as you progress—performance can be intoxicating; the more you get, the more you want—take the time at each step to determine the result you're looking for. Analyze the changes you have in mind to see if they're likely to meet your new goal. Don't proceed until you're convinced they will.

4

Building from a solid base

Since the point of modifying a car is to make it handle better or accelerate quicker or stop surer or look sharper, the car you're working with ought to be in top condition to begin with. Otherwise, the improvements may do no more than make up for existing problems, and the overall gain would be zero. While some folks can undertake performance projects with new or nearly new Hondas, many cannot. So except for those with showroom-fresh cars, a thorough inspection will be necessary, which in turn will show what service or repairs are required.

Body

Start with the body, even if you're working on a car you've owned several years; familiarity sometimes leads to acceptance of small problems that added together can affect performance. The two main concerns are body straightness and structural rust. They are important because Hondas are unibody cars without frames; the bodyshell gives the car its strength. If the car has been badly wrecked and then poorly repaired, the bodyshell may be bent, making wheel alignment impossible. The result will be poor or inconsistent handling, or excessive tire wear. Structural rust—rust at points of the body important for strength, like the cowl and suspension attachment points—is detrimental for similar reasons. The suspension needs a solid base to work against. If its supports are weakened by rust, the body bends as the suspension moves. This can alter alignment and sap the strength of the suspension's springs, shock absorbers and anti-roll bars.

In looking for wreck-related body damage, start at the top of the car and work downward. Are the surfaces of the roof and tops of the fenders smooth? Look for a slight wrinkle or wave in the metal; look

The two Jackson Racing-prepared Team GRR Hondas—numbers 42 and 43—wrap up the 1988 Escort Endurance championship during the year's final race in Sebring, Florida. The team repeated its championship in 1989.

from different directions as the angle of light can mask imperfections. Check out the hood, doors and hatch or trunk lid as well, but remember that these easily changed parts are often replaced rather than repaired. Even so, they should fit their openings well; Honda is known for precise alignment of body parts. Look down the sides of the car carefully. They may have dings from rocks or doors being opened on them but again, look for the serious sort of damage that leaves ripples. Generally, expect the smooth contours you'd find on a showroom demonstrator or be suspicious. Under the hood, along the inner fenders and around the struts, look for wrinkles and kinks as well. These inner areas often are not as well finished by body shops, and may hold the only clue to structural damage.

While waves and wrinkles on the outer surface can be hard to detect, rust is a blemish that brags its presence to anyone in shouting range. Depending on its location, the rust can be a nuisance to be repaired as a simple cosmetic improvement—say, when custom bodywork is added and painted, or if the whole car is being painted. But at its worst, rust can render the unibody too weak for performance use or even general use. From the outside, search for rust where the windshield pillars attach to the body. On certain Hondas, particularly notchbacks like Preludes, check the rear pillars as well. The point is that the roof and its supports give the body much of its torsional stiffness, the ability to resist twisting. The pillars and roof tie the large opening for the passenger compartment together, so they must be strong.

Other common spots for rust are at the bottom of the fenders or corners of the doors where water can collect. They generally do not affect the structure unless the rust has spread from the outer sheet metal to the underlying bodyshell. However, heavy rust in the rocker panels—can indicate serious weakness that allows the body to sag front to rear. Doors that are hard to open or close, or that do not align with their openings can confirm this sort of damage.

Inspecting the structure underneath is just as important. Look at the bumpers to see if they are straight and sit evenly. Then look underneath them. If necessary, jack up the car. Place it on safety stands before getting underneath. See if the bumper supports have been bent and then straightened. If so, see if the body structure for these supports has been bent as well; follow the trail as far as you can. A front or rear hit, if it's hard enough, can result in the unibody being bent enough to move the suspension attachment points, affecting wheel alignment. Also look for rust underneath the car, particularly around the brackets for the suspension components and at the front of the floor pan where it bends upward to meet the firewall. Remember that the sheet metal serves as the car's frame and rust can rob its strength.

In some cases, structural rust can be repaired by welding in new metal or a replacement body section from Honda. But, if the rust is extensive, it's probably better to buy another car. Repair of structural rust should be left to an established body repair shop with experience in this complicated, safety related work. Such a shop could be useful in evaluating the condition of the body: whether to repair it or replace it.

The same is true for evaluating a car that has been wrecked. If you find body damage, have the car checked on a four-wheel alignment rack. Hondas generally have few wheel-alignment adjustments, so if the car cannot be aligned, the only remedy is frame straightening. On a frame-straightening machine, the unibody can be bent back into shape—racing teams use such body jigs to coax the wheels into the most desirable settings—but there are limits. Again, find a reputable, well-equipped body shop and ask its advice.

Suspension

After confirming the body to be sound and straight, move on to the individual chassis components. Unless the car is new or nearly new, they should be checked one by one. In the same way that the suspension needs a strong structure to work against, each component must be able to carry its load. Fitting alloy wheels and high-performance tires to a car with bad wheel bearings, for instance, would be like buying top-notch track shoes for a runner with sprained ankles. Each link in the chain must be at full strength before increasing the pressure through the addition of high-performance components. If you find worn parts, you may wish to buy high-performance replacements. These choices are discussed in the following chapters.

Inspect each part one by one. Some suspension parts like bushings can be checked visually for good condition, but others like wheel bearings or ball joints may require a service manual for reference. The factory manuals, which may be bought through Honda dealers, are the most complete. It's often good to have a second manual, however, that explains procedures in terms that others besides dealer mechanics understand; the Haynes series is a good example.

A number of general tests can be used, in any case. For instance, testing struts or shock absorbers by bouncing each corner of the car one at a time will give a reasonable reading of each unit's damping ability. Push down on a fender and bounce the car several times. Then stop. The car should not bounce more than one additional cycle. If it does, the strut or shock at that corner is probably worn out. Another indication of a bad strut or shock is fluid leakage where the rod enters the body of the strut or shock. All suspension bushings (in control arms, on anti-roll bars and so on) should appear solid. They should not be cracked or torn looking, or severely dried out. Those that are should be replaced.

Wheel bearings, ball joints and tie-rod ends must be checked differently. Some problems with these components will show up on a road test. For instance, if the car pulls strongly to one side under acceleration, look for a bad tie rod.

For a thorough check, though, the car should be jacked up and on safety stands. First, check the sealing boots on the joints. They should not be torn or ruptured in any way. Joints with bad boots should be replaced. If the boots are good, these components generally can be further checked by grabbing the tire at the nine o'clock and three o'clock positions and wiggling it left or right. There should be no looseness. At the front, you should be able to steer the wheel left or right, but there should be resistance. Any unresisted movement—it may be minute, showing up only with slight left-right movement of the tire—should be tracked down. Do this by first looking at the tie rod. Does it move as soon as the tire moves, or is there lag? If there is lag, the tie rod should be replaced. If not, look at the ball joint. Is there any looseness there? The upright should pivot around the joint as the wheel is turned left and right, but there should be no wobbling or movement side to side. If there is, the ball joint should be replaced. If not, look at the upright. Does it move as soon as the tire does? If there is lag between tire movement and upright movement, the wheel bearing is bad and should be replaced. Sometimes grabbing the wheel at the twelve o'clock and six o'clock positions and trying to wobble the tire from top to bottom will point out ball joint or wheel bearing trouble as well.

The same procedures apply to the rear wheels, except that on all Hondas but the four-wheel-steer Prelude there is no steering mechanism. This eliminates a variable and makes tracking down any looseness one step easier. Generally, if there is suspension looseness at any corner of the car, it's a fairly straightforward matter to tug on the tire and track down the slack.

Steering

The same sort of approach applies to the steering system as was used for the suspension. In this

Cleaning and refurbishing vital components such as those that make up the suspension are important parts of preparing a car for high-performance use. The immaculate right front suspension of Angelo Roberson's Honda Civic 1200 shows this attention to detail.

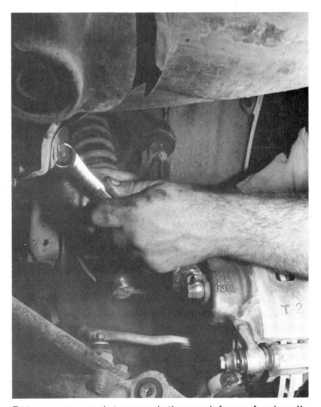
Between-race maintenance is thorough for professionally raced Hondas like the Jackson Racing-prepared CRXs for SCCA Escort Endurance Racing. The suspension components are among those thoroughly inspected. Nothing is excepted: "Things that wear out on the car—any moving part—is looked at," Jackson says. "Tie rod ends, bushings wear out, ball joints wear out. Those are things that are important to check. We check all the hubs and bearings to make sure everything is 100 percent."

case, with the car on the ground, move the steering wheel left and right. There should be no looseness; you should feel resistance from the tires immediately. If there is slack, begin tracing it from the steering wheel on down. The steering column bearings must be in good condition. You should not be able to move the steering wheel up or down, or side to side. If they are tight, have someone rock the steering wheel back and forth lightly and check the universal joints on the steering shaft; look under the dash and under the hood. Any lag between an upper part of the shaft and the shaft below a universal joint indicates a bad joint. If there is a lag between the shaft where it enters the steering rack and movement of the tie rods, then the looseness is within the rack. If so, check your service manual for adjustments, or rebuild or replace it.

Brakes

The ability of a car to stop is a vital part of its handling, and braking effectiveness is influenced by time and mileage more than nearly any other performance aspect. So, even if your car is just a year or two old, some maintenance may be required. For instance, Honda recommends replacement of the brake fluid for many of its models every 30,000 miles.

Brake fluid, particularly in humid climates, absorbs water from the air which hurts braking performance two ways. First, moisture corrodes the

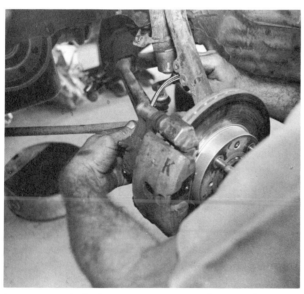

Improvements between races are made as well. In this case, the stock synthetic-rubber brake hoses are replaced with steel-braided hoses for greater durability and firmer brake pedal feel.

master cylinder, drum brake wheel cylinders, steel brake lines and the cylinders of disk brake calipers. Second, it lowers the temperature at which the fluid will boil. This is important, because when the brakes are used hard they become hot, in turn heating the fluid in the wheel cylinders and brake calipers, and nearby brake lines. This heat can boil deteriorated brake fluid, causing you to have to push the pedal farther for a given amount of braking, or lengthening the pedal travel so greatly that the car will not stop.

Hydraulic brake systems, as used by Honda and all other modern cars, rely on brake components full of brake fluid and devoid of any sort of bubbles—whether from air or vapor from boiled fluid. So, if your car has some miles on it and has not had the brakes bled recently, consider doing so. If it has a hydraulically actuated clutch, bleed it as well.

There are several methods for bleeding the systems, and some tools allow a single person to do the work. If you use one, just follow the instructions. Otherwise, use a helper to pump the brake pedal. First, fill the brake master cylinder with fresh, top-quality fluid (brake fluid that sits in a partially empty container for a long period can absorb moisture just as fluid in the car can). Obtain a pint-sized container to catch the fluid, and a small hose about a foot long, that will fit over the nipples of the brake bleeders. The bleeders are found near the top of disk brake calipers and at the back of drum brake wheel cylinders.

Depending on the model, the car may need to be jacked up and the wheels may need to be removed. If so, use safety stands and make sure your helper is careful not to rock the car. Start at the rear with the cylinder or caliper farthest from the master cylinder. Crack the bleeder open (use a wrench to turn it about a half-turn counterclockwise) to make sure it is free and then immediately close it. Then have your helper pump the brake pedal three or four times. At your command, have the helper stop pumping and hold pressure on the pedal at the top of the stroke. With the hose attached to the bleeder and the far end in the container, open the bleeder and let fluid flow into the container until your helper says the brake pedal has reached the floor. Have the helper hold the pedal on the floor until you close the bleeder. At your command, the helper should then release the pedal. Repeat the process until the fluid entering the container is clear, indicating that fresh fluid now stretches from the master cylinder to the wheel cylinder or caliper you just bled. Refill the master cylinder with fresh fluid and move on to the other rear wheel and repeat the process. Then move to the front. Add more fluid and bleed the front brake farthest from the master cylinder. Add fluid again and bleed the remaining brake. Top off the master cylinder with fluid one more time.

Once the car is back on the ground and the engine is running, pump the brakes several times. Once this has been done, there should be little play in the brake pedal; there should be firm resistance after a short movement of the pedal. Dispose of the used fluid properly.

If there still is play in the brake pedal, several checks may be required. If the car has rear drum brakes, they may be out of adjustment (disk brakes need no adjustment). The adjustment of the brake pedal stop, or the rod between it and the power brake booster may be incorrect. Follow the instructions in the service manual for your model in making these adjustments, or have a repair shop do so.

If the play remains, and particularly if it increases, the master cylinder, a wheel cylinder or a caliper could be leaking. Inspect these components or have a shop do so. A word of caution on brake bleeding: If the fluid has absorbed a lot of moisture and has corroded the master cylinder badly, the act of pumping the cylinder through its full travel may ruin

The brakes themselves are among the items rebuilt between races. Here the rear brakes of an Escort Endurance CRX Si are readied for replacement.

its piston seals and cause it to leak. While it's true that the master cylinder might last longer in such a case if not bled, the possible damage to it indicates brake system trouble that will lead to failure sooner or later.

Several other brake parts should be inspected as well; disk brake pads and drum brake shoes, for instance. They must have sufficient brake material on them to work properly; they must not have reached minimum thickness. Additionally, the surface of the brake disk or drum must be sufficiently smooth; deep scoring will hurt brake performance. Follow service manual instructions for inspection or have a shop do so.

Finally, the flexible hoses used to bridge the variable gaps between the chassis and the brakes should be inspected. Hoses should be replaced if they are cracked, chipped or show signs of having rubbed against another component. Also, you should consider replacing hoses on older or high-mileage cars even if they appear all right. After long use, the hoses sometimes will break down internally. The result is either a constriction that slows the flow of brake fluid or a tear that creates a check valve of sorts that allows fluid to pass in just one direction. Then that brake either cannot be applied or will not release. So, consider replacing old brake hoses on principle just as you might replace a still-serviceable radiator hose because of age.

Clutch, transaxle and CV joints

Inspection and maintenance of the driveline is straightforward. And, for the most part, the axiom that it either works or it doesn't. When one of these parts begins to fail, it will usually go all the way, quickly. When you consider that all the power of the engine must be transmitted through the clutch, transaxle and then the constant velocity joints, this makes sense.

There are useful preventive measures that should be undertaken regularly, however. The intervals are spelled out in the car's owners and service manuals. Clutch adjustment should be checked regularly. As the clutch wears, free play in the clutch pedal diminishes. Eventually, if the free play is not adjusted, it will be as if the car is driven with the clutch pedal partially depressed. The clutch will begin slipping and will wear out quickly.

Several driving tips will lengthen a clutch's life: never rest your foot on the pedal as you're driving; hold the car against an incline with the brakes, rather than the clutch and engine; and put the transaxle in neutral for long stops and release the clutch, rather than leaving the car in gear and holding the clutch pedal down. From stoplight to stoplight over tens of thousands of miles, this can make a great difference in the durability of the clutch-release bearing and pressure plate.

The main upkeep for the transaxle is checking its oil level from time to time, and changing the oil at the recommended intervals. Most importantly, use the type and weight oil recommended by Honda for your model.

There really is no procedure for maintaining constant velocity joints. However, it's smart to inspect their boots from time to time for cracks, breaks or cuts. If you catch a boot just as it ruptures, you can save the joint by replacing the boot. But if a constant velocity joint is exposed for even a short time, dirt will ruin it. Otherwise, as long as the joints are quiet—worn constant velocity joints will clack loudly in turns—they probably are in good condition.

Engine ancillaries

These ancillary components, some of which are also called accessories such as alternators and power steering pumps, must also be in top condition for performance use. Inspection is straightforward and Honda's maintenance schedule should be followed. In the case of an alternator, power steering pump or water pump, make sure the engine is off, and then grab the pulley for each component and try to wobble it from side to side. There should be no play. For some Honda engines, the water pump pulley is driven by the camshaft belt and cannot be easily reached. There should be no leakage from the pumps; the power steering pump should be topped off as should the cooling system. With the engine running, the hood open and your hands, clothing and hair a safe distance from the engine, listen for any grinding or rumbling noises from these components. There should be none.

Other ancillary parts include the engine's belts, hoses and filters. V-belts driving parts like the alternator, air conditioner compressor or power steering pump should be checked with the engine off. There should be no glazing along the belts' sides—which are the surfaces that contact the pulleys, and absorb

Keeping filters clean and working properly is one of the keys to long engine life. Oscar Jackson of Jackson Racing shows that air filters with rubber or plastic facings can cause the low air filter seal to break away from the hous-ing. For this reason, Jackson recommends Honda filters, which have metal facings that are compatible with the housing's seals.

Jackson is also a proponent of Honda oil filters. On the left he holds a Honda filter and on the right he holds an aftermarket filter. Jackson says cutting the filters open shows metal components in the Honda filter versus cardboard equivalents in the aftermarket filter, indicating that the Honda part is of higher quality.

power from one pulley and pass it on to the next. The belts should not be cracked or appear dried out. They should be pliable and look nearly new.

Cooling system hoses should have similar characteristics. Check them with the engine off and while they're cold. Their neoprene should be pliable, but not mushy; there should be no cracks and there should be no bloated areas. Because of variance in climate and use, it's difficult to state an age or mileage when cooling hoses should be replaced, but at some point for older Hondas it makes sense to change them as a set, probably during a routine replacement of the antifreeze coolant.

Following Honda's schedule for replacing coolant is important not only because it keeps the engine from freezing in cold weather and boiling over in hot weather, but because it has anti-corrosive agents that protect aluminum engine parts. The fuel system also uses hoses that should be replaced if any sign of deterioration appears or simply as a preventive measure once the car gets older. Because of the fire hazard a leaking fuel hose can create, if you have any doubt, replace the hose.

Fuel, oil and air filters should be replaced at least as often as Honda recommends, as should the engine oil. Honda claims its oil filters have features that filters from other suppliers do not have, and many Honda shops recommend their use. In carbureted

The timing belt is a part that should be inspected periodically, and replaced whenever there is any question of its condition. Here, the upper belt is new and can be identified by the sharply cut corners on its teeth. The lower belt has 28,000 miles on it and could be reused, even though the teeth show a bit of rounding on their corners. A belt should be replaced if it is cracked, oily or has severely rounded teeth. Belts from the 1973 through 1983 Civics, and the 1488, 1597 and 1751 CVCC engines can last as long as the engine under certain circumstances. However, the belts on later engines are much more prone to breaking, which can bend valves and break pistons. In any case, inspect and replace the timing belt at least as often as recommended by the car's owner manual or service manual.

Hondas, the metal-edged air filters supplied by Honda should be used rather than the plastic-edged filters often sold. The plastic seems to pull loose the rubber seals in the bottom and top of the air filter canister and leads to leakage, according to Honda specialist Oscar Jackson of Jackson Racing in Huntington Beach, California. I've observed this phenomenon as well. Do not skimp on filters or oil. Buy top-quality products that meet Honda's requirements and change them often.

The engine for a professional race car gets as much attention as anything. This cylinder for a 1988 CRX Si has been honed carefully and awaits cleaned-up pistons and new piston rings. Jackson Racing uses a rigid hone with manually positioned stones to ensure straight cylinders.

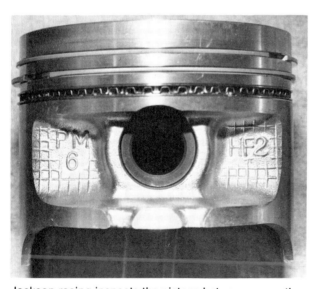

Jackson racing inspects the pistons between races, then cleans them and installs new rings, being careful to make sure the rings' gaps are properly staggered to prevent excess compression blow-by. This work is done after an engine racks up twelve hours of use. "We look for things like how much color there is below the top rings to see how well the rings have been sealing," Jackson says.

Engine

Jackson, whose Hondas have won several national racing championships, and who prepared the Honda CRXs that won the Showroom Stock B manufacturer's championship for the SCCA Escort Endurance races in 1988, goes through the full list of inspections between each race. The engines are also disassembled, inspected and rebuilt after relatively short periods of racing use; their time on the track is carefully logged for reference. While this strict schedule of engine rebuilding is unreasonable for even the most sincere non-professional enthusiast, the principle behind it—that every component must give its all—is not. This applies particularly to the engine, the heart of the car. And while a strong engine cannot make a high-performance car by itself, neither can a car perform well with a weak engine.

The tune of the engine, that is, the condition of the spark plugs, the setting of the ignition timing,

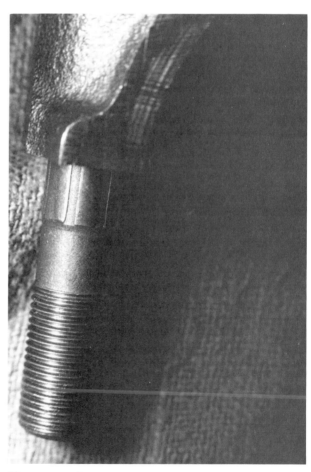

The connecting rod bolts are important for durability. Many engine builders replace them every time they take an engine apart, particularly when rules require the use of stock bolts.

the adjustment of the valves and so on, is important, and the engine should be tuned at least as often as Honda recommends. But for high-performance use, the overall condition of the engine should be determined as well. Common sense says that an engine with 100,000 miles or more on it should be rebuilt if it is to be driven hard, even though a Honda engine with that mileage may have plenty of life remaining for general use.

Engines that could be called middle-aged, say in the 40,000 to 60,000 mile range, are more difficult to evaluate. Much depends on how hard they've been driven, how well they've been maintained and the conditions to which they've been subjected. For instance, in looking for a used Honda, Jackson often prefers a car that has relatively high freeway mileage to a car with relatively low stop-and-go city mileage. The steady pace of the highway can be easier on an engine, and the car as a whole, than the bump and grind of the city streets.

So, with mileage such an imprecise criterion, several tests should be made. The first involves removing the valve cover or at least its oil filler cap. Look inside. While the oil may be dark in color or even black, it should all be liquid. There should be no congealed, gooey-looking oil. Sludge or dry flakes of oil residue indicate that the engine has not been well cared for. It may have been used in stop-and-go driving and without the additional oil changes that such conditions call for, or under normal conditions with oil changing badly neglected, or it may have been overheated. Any engine like this is a poor candidate for high-performance use, even if other tests show it to be relatively sound.

Other simple indications that an engine needs rebuilding include blue smoke from the exhaust; this indicates oil burning. Excessive oil use, even if no smoke is noticeable, is also an indication. A quart of oil ought to last more than 1,000 miles, although hard driving can decrease this a bit, but an engine that uses more than a quart of oil per 500 miles under almost any condition needs rebuilding.

Noises from within the engine may indicate a rebuild. A clicking or tapping from the top of the engine may indicate nothing more than the need for valve adjustment, but a deeper knocking or pounding noise from the lower part of the engine could be serious and indicate a bad connecting rod bearing or main crankshaft bearing. An engine whose oil light flickers at idle or oil gauge reads low may be a candidate for rebuilding. Install a mechanical oil pressure gauge to confirm this first, however.

Two other tests are good indicators of an engine's condition. They both reveal the ability of the

piston rings and valves to seal against the cylinder walls and valve seats. No engine with significant leakage at one of these points will run well. Good compression sealing is one of the keys to high power output, and one of the main reasons for frequent rebuilding of racing engines.

The first procedure is the compression test. For this, a compression tester (a pressure gauge that reads in pounds per square inch and has adaptors to mate with the spark plug holes) must be used. Remove the spark plugs. Install the gauge in the first plug hole. Make sure your hands, clothes and hair are away from any rotating parts of the engine and from

With the connecting rods out of the engine, they are cleaned and inspected. The big-end bore is carefully inspected for signs of metal transfer. Such evidence would show that a bearing had tried to spin, sticking to the crankshaft and rotating in the rod, rather than standing firm in the rod and allowing the crank to rotate within the bearing.

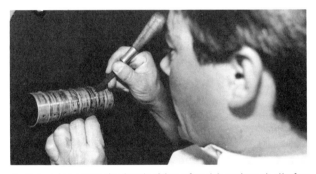

Jackson inspects the back sides of rod-bearing shells for evidence of metal transfer as well. "We'll look at them and ask: 'Do I have any abnormalities here? Is any one worse than another one?'" Jackson says. Looking closely at one of the shells, Jackson says: "This one here seems to be slightly scuffed, a little bit more than the rest—but nothing that's damaging. But it's something that's important to look at."

the ends of the ignition wires. Have a helper hold the throttle open and turn the engine over with the starter for about a half-dozen revolutions. Note the reading. Repeat the procedure for each cylinder.

Honda lists compression specifications in its service manuals. But while the engine should meet these figures, variance in accuracy between different compression gauges have led some manufacturers and mechanics to follow another standard: less than fifteen percent difference between the readings for the highest and lowest cylinders. For example, if the best cylinder reads 180 pounds per square inch, the worst should read no less than 153 pounds per square inch. If a compression test leaves any question (particularly low or varied readings), the next test should be performed.

A cylinder leak-down test is the second and most accurate procedure for checking an engine's ability to keep the air-fuel mixture within the cylinders while it's being compressed and burned. A leak-down tester and an air compressor are required. Like a compression gauge, a leak-down tester requires removal of the spark plugs and insertion—cylinder by cylinder—of an adaptor into each spark plug hole. Unlike a compression test, however, the engine is not turned over with the starter. Instead, the cylinder to which the tester is attached must be brought to top dead center—meaning that the piston is at the top of the cylinder, having just finished its upward exhaust stroke and being ready to begin its downward intake stroke.

The tester is a gauge and pressure regulator that attaches to the engine adaptor on one end and air compressor on the other. Use the regulator to "zero" the gauge—make it read a leakage of zero percent—by attaching the compressor and then closing the passage to the engine. Once the passage is opened, the gauge will read the compression leakage. The ideal figure, of course, would be zero percent. But, in practice, a reading of two or three percent is considered proper for a well-built, freshly broken-in engine. For a used engine, leakage of five percent or less is good. If a cylinder reads ten percent or more, the leakage is significant and should be tracked down.

Luckily, this bit of sleuthing is elementary. Leave the pressurized tester attached to the bad cylinder. Remove the air filter, the oil filler cap and the radiator cap (the engine and cooling system must be cold). If you hear air hissing into the air filter housing, the culprit is a leaking intake valve. If air can

Of course, Jackson inspects the bearing surface as well. "The top half of the bearing is the one that takes the most beating," he says. "It's the one that gets fired and slammed down on the top of the crank."

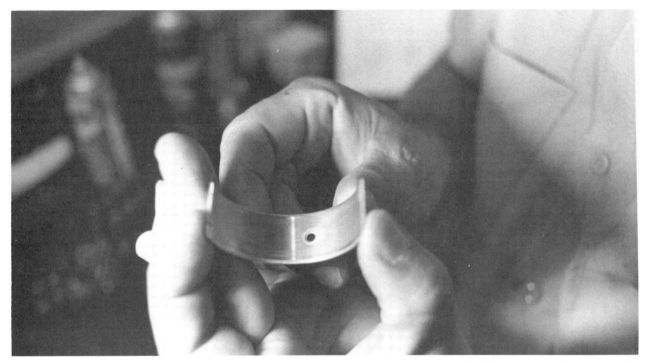

The bottom bearing shell catches the rod "as it's heading to the top and keeps it from going out," Jackson says. "In a desperation situation, if your bearings are looking bad and you're at a race and you don't know what to do, you can flip them over—change sides."

The fit of a new bearing shell must be exact and its surface must be perfectly smooth.

be heard or felt exiting the filler, the problem is the seal between the piston rings and cylinder wall. The rings could be worn or broken, or the cylinder wall could be worn or scored. If bubbles can be seen rising from the coolant, the head gasket is bad, or there is a crack in the cylinder head or block. If the leaking air fails to appear at any of these places, walk to the back of the car and investigate one other possibility—the exhaust. Air escaping from the exhaust pipe indicates a leaking exhaust valve.

As you can see, any leakage of this magnitude will require at least partial disassembly of the engine to rectify. In the case of a bad intake or exhaust valve, the cylinder head must be removed and a valve job will be required.

Taking the head off for valve work allows you to inspect the cylinders as well. This can be done several ways. First, the surface of the cylinders should be

Mark DiBella of Jackson Racing uses a piston-ring compressor and a wooden hammer handle to tap a piston into place in one of the Escort Endurance CRX Si engines. Oscar Jackson guides the connecting rod into position, paying particular attention to the rod bolts to ensure that a bolt does not gouge the crankshaft journal. When working alone, cutting a couple of lengths of fuel hose and sticking them over the bolts will help protect the crankshaft.

smooth, although the cross-hatched pattern of the factory cylinder honing may still be vaguely visible. Second, sliding a feeler gauge between the pistons and cylinders will give a close approximation of the piston-to-cylinder clearance. Third, if you have the equipment, use of an inside micrometer will indicate whether the cylinders have worn, or become out-of-round or tapered. Check your service manual for limits on wear, roundness and taper.

In the case of leakage into the coolant, the head must also be removed for inspection. If the head gasket was the cause, the trail usually will be apparent. However, head gasket failures are often brought on by warped cylinder heads or block decks. The remnants of the head gasket must be scraped and completely cleaned off (take care not to mar any surfaces that mate with the gasket; aluminum is particularly easy to gouge). Once this is done, check the head and deck for flatness. Use a straightedge on both surfaces; there should be no gaps between it, and the head or deck. Also, the surfaces should be smooth with no pitting. If you have any doubts, seek assistance from a mechanic or engine machine shop. If the surfaces prove flat, look for cracks. Often they will be hard to find and may require the help of a mechanic or engine machinist.

In the case of leakage past the piston rings, an engine rebuild is required. For engines that will be kept in relatively stock condition (stock compression pistons, and stock or mildly reground camshafts), rebuild the engine to stock specifications using stock replacement parts. Builders of Showroom Stock racing engines do this regularly, using Honda parts exclusively, and find the engines extremely reliable, even in endurance racing. The best rule of thumb when rebuilding and remachining an engine is to shoot for the exact clearances recommended by Honda in its service manuals, even though Honda allows some tolerance above and below the desired figures. Racing engine builders vary slightly from the specifications for small gains in power through friction reduction or increased piston ring sealing, and in the width, location and angles ground on valves and valve seats. But these hard-learned sizing secrets are closely guarded confidences.

The Honda specifications are quite good, however; do not allow a machinist or engine builder unfamiliar with Hondas to talk you into drastic variations in clearances. The old adage that a loose engine—one whose clearances are greater than stock—will make greater power does not apply to Hondas. The clearances appear tight to those used to working with larger engines, but Honda parts are precise and are intended to be used with minimal clearance. You can gain power simply by remachining and rebuilding an engine exactly to Honda's specifications; this process is called blueprinting. The term means that the engine matches the design blueprints exactly.

Balancing the engine's reciprocating parts (the pistons and connecting rods) of the engine along with certain rotating parts like the crankshaft and flywheel won't bring more power, but could result in a smoother-running engine. The smoothness in turn leads to greater longevity. The work must be carried out on a special balancing machine and not all engine shops offer the service. For an engine rebuilt from stock components, balancing often is unnecessary. However, it is good insurance.

5

Preparing for more power

Eking out one horsepower here and two horsepower there through precise blueprinting is about the only way to increase the power of a competition engine constrained by Showroom Stock specifications. On the other hand, engines freed from these constraints demand additional preparation. Such engines—destined for street cars in which the owner sets the performance parameters, or upper-level racing in which engine-modification rules are liberal—will not survive high-horsepower pounding without a thorough strengthening regimen.

To chronicle the additional preparation needed for modified engines and further examine the blueprinting process, I followed the machining and assembly of a modified street engine by RC Engineering for a 1984 CRX. RC Engineering of Torrance, California, is an engine building company that, like Jackson Racing, has helped carry the flag for Honda on the professional road racing circuits. At RC, I talked to founder Russ Collins who is well-known in motorcycling for his Honda-powered drag racers, and to two of his engine builders, brothers Kenny and Tom Deagle. Kenny builds short-blocks (all of the engine except the cylinder head) while Tom builds cylinder heads. I also talked to Oscar Jackson, whose company, besides preparing the CRXs that won the 1988 SCCA Escort Endurance Championship, is one of the leading Honda engine-component suppliers and builds modified engines on request.

As could be expected from two competitors, opinions varied on specific components and procedures, but their tenets for producing more power are the same: the insistence on straight, round cylinders; precisely ground valves and seats; and strict control of clearances between the pistons and cylinders, and the bearings and crankshaft.

Some enthusiasts have the background, perseverance and tools to approach the engine-building abilities of these Honda specialists. Many, however,

do not. If you plan an engine rebuild, a good way to choose between a homebuilt engine and a professionally built engine is to study the photographs and descriptions in this chapter and the preceding chapter. Then judge your ability to carry out each step. The work is painstaking. "You really need a machine shop," Collins says, to properly fit the parts to one another. "Some people don't know you can do these things, much less be able to do them."

Still, with the help of a local engine machinist, some enthusiasts can approach the race-level quality of these shops. Others are capable of rebuilding certain portions of the engine but should ship the rest out to a specialist. But for many, the whole process is overwhelming. In making this assessment, remember that money saved by doing the work at home is of value only if engine performance and longevity are not compromised.

Connecting rods

The rods are the components about which RC Engineering and Jackson Racing appear to differ the most. RC advocates heat-treating them so they will resist bending, and shot-peening them to forestall cracking. Kenny Deagle sets up a dramatic test to demonstrate the difference between a stock rod and a heat-treated rod. He places the big end of the stock rod in a vice and wedges a long lever in the small end. He begins twisting the rod. There is little resistance, and he continues to twist the small end until the rod looks like a licorice stick. The same test performed on a heat-treated rod results in a hard battle to put a slight bend in the rod's shank.

This is not the point, says Oscar Jackson. The key, he says, is that the heat-treating process requires the rods to be straightened and thoroughly remachined. Jackson says he's found stock Honda rods to be reliable, and questions whether the machine tools of an engine shop can produce a rod as straight and accurately machined as those produced on the Honda factory machine tools.

Whichever approach is taken, the rods must be straight, their bores must meet Honda size tolerances and the bolts should be replaced.

In RC's engine, the rods are heat-treated and shot-peened, so several hours are spent straightening the rods, and resizing their ends with a special honing machine and other tools.

Crankshaft

The crankshaft can be lightened to increase the engine's capability to accelerate, and its counterweights can be shaped to slice through the crankcase's oil with less resistance. Both procedures are undertaken on RC's engine, with two pounds being machined off the counterweights, and the counterweights being knife-edged to cut the oil. These modifications require the crankshaft to be rebalanced. The bearing surfaces are also machined and polished.

A machined-down Honda flywheel—lightened by three pounds on a lathe—complements the lightened crankshaft, further reducing the engine's rotational weight and increasing engine acceleration.

Like Jackson Racing, RC Engineering builds a number of hot Honda engines for street use in addition to Showroom Stock racing engines. In doing so, RC spends much time on machining and heat treating engine components for exact fit and durability. To prove the worth of heat treating and shot peening connecting rods, RC's Kenny Deagle sets up this test with a treated rod in the rear of the vise and an untreated rod in the front.

Deagle uses a pry bar through the small ends of the rods to show their resistance to bending. The treated rod, top, springs back when tension is released.

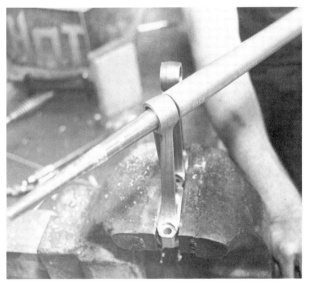

The untreated rod, bottom, remains bent.

By continuing to pry against the rod, Deagle is able to twist it 180 degrees.

The treated rod, on the other hand, battles back and cannot be twisted more than 45 degrees or so. The importance of the test is that the heat treating makes the connecting rods more resilient to the pounding of continual high-power output.

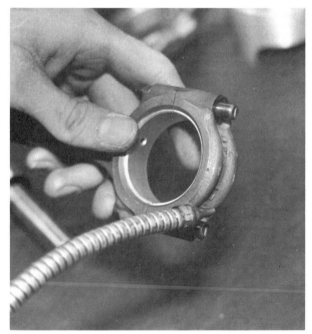

Before assembly for initial measurement, the bolts of this rod are lubricated. RC prefers Mobil 1 synthetic engine oil or engine-assembly oil. The parts are from a carbureted 1984 CRX engine 1488 engine that will be converted to CRX Si specifications with a non-CVCC cylinder head. The engine is intended for high-performance street use, and need not meet the requirements of any racing rules.

Connecting rods that will be used in an engine are treated with care, measured and remeasured, cleaned and recleaned.

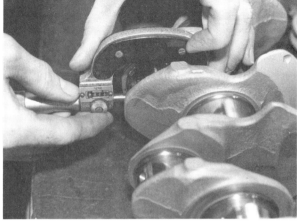

The journal that the particular rod will be used on is first measured with a micrometer.

The nuts' tightness is measured with a bolt-stretch gauge rather than a torque wrench. The gauge measures the amount the bolt stretches as it's tightened down. This method is considered superior by RC Engineering, Jackson Racing and others because it is not subject to variations in lubrication or friction from mating threads as a reading from a torque wrench is. However, bolt stretch can only be measured on a bolt whose head and end are in the open like a rod bolt's, so torque wrenches are used elsewhere.

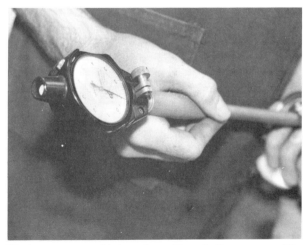

That measurement is transferred to a dial bore gauge. The gauge reads the clearance between the bearing and the journal in thousandths of an inch.

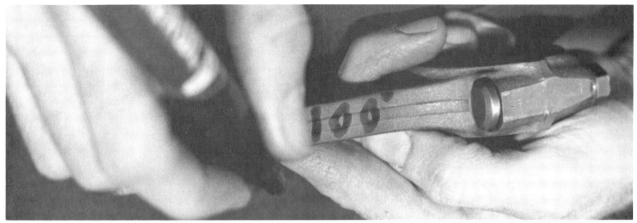

If an adjustment in bore size is required, the amount of change is noted on the side of the connecting rod with a marker.

A gauge, calibrated with a micrometer, is used to measure the size of the connecting rod's big-end bore. It should read zero, plus or minus 0.0002 in., when the machining is completed.

To resize the rod, it is placed on a honing machine that is specially configured for the work. The big end of the connecting rod is honed to the desired diameter.

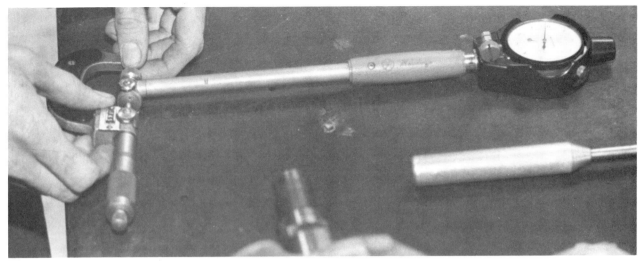

The crankshaft journal and connecting rod are measured again to confirm the desired clearance.

If the crankshaft has a journal that is slightly undersize—but not so far to require remachining—the big end of the connecting rod is made smaller to compensate. That is the case with one journal and rod in this engine. The rod is first placed sideways in a hydraulic press; a foot-pedal controls the pressure exerted on the rod.

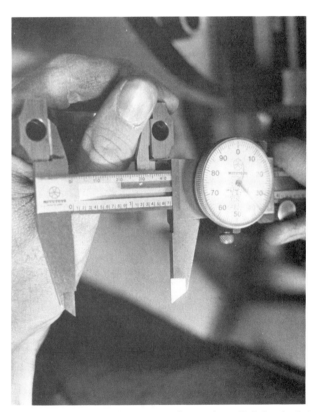

The end of the rod is squeezed together slightly. A dial caliper is used to see if the rod is within the size range desired.

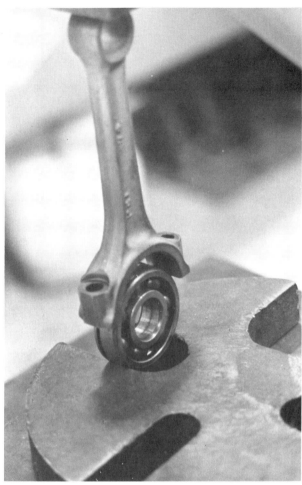

If the target is overshot, the end of the rod must be re-opened a bit. Using the press, and an old bearing as a mandrel, the rod end is spread.

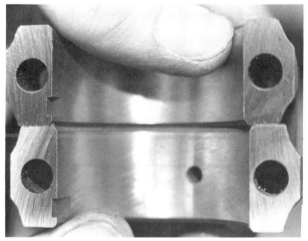

Once these preliminary diameter-shrinking operations are completed, both with the connecting rod and the rod cap, the rod is nearly ready for honing.

The mating face of the rod must be machined as well to keep the big end concentric. The rod cap will be refaced in this cap grinder.

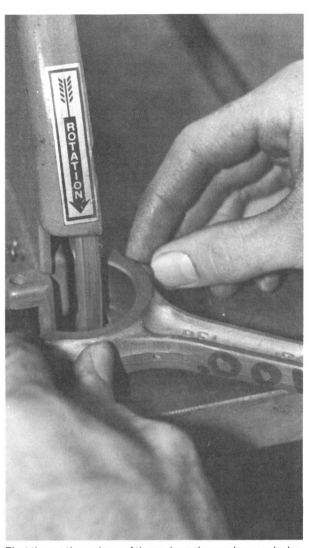

First the mating edges of the rod are dressed on a grinder.

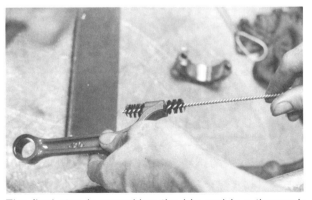

The final step in reworking the big end is a thorough cleaning. Of the process, Deagle says: "We can safely resize a rod two times. Then you have to look for another one, because moving it up and down starts to work-harden it and you'll get a stressed area."

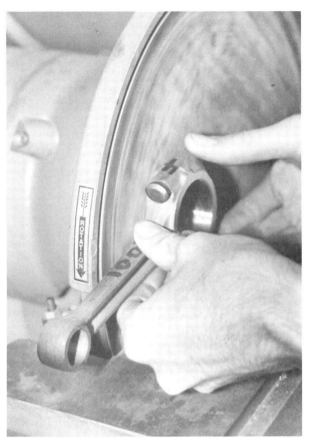

Then the rod is reassembled and rehoned to final size; its big end is made round again. Then the sides of the big end are dressed on a grinder.

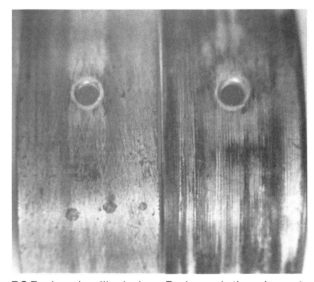

RC Engineering, like Jackson Racing and others, inspects both sides of used connecting-rod bearings to see how their work holds up under competition.

Once sized, RC's heat-treated rods must be checked for straightness because the heat can make the rod sag slightly, Deagle says.

This is first done with a height gauge with the rod lying on a granite base.

If the height of the small end differs from side to side, the rod must be straightened. When required, the initial straightening is done on a hydraulic with an aluminum block protecting the beam of the rod, and flattened bearing inserts protecting the ends.

To make the final check for straightness, the piston must be installed on the rod. First, the wrist pin is polished on a lathe with a fine grade of sandpaper.

Then the wrist pin bores of the piston are honed to fit the pin exactly.

The diameter is judged by resistance offered to the pin as it is pushed into the piston.

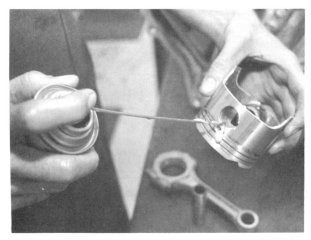

To prepare for installing the piston on the rod, Deagle lubricates its wrist pin bores with engine-assembly oil.

The wrist pin is pressed into the connecting rod; an interference fit between the pin and rod retains the pin.

The pin rotates in the bores of the piston and the aluminum of the piston is the bearing material.

Once fitted with pistons, the connecting rods are placed into a jig for measuring straightness.

If such a gap is detected, the rod must be further straightened. This is done by placing the rod in a vice and bending it slightly with a pry bar. The rod and piston are then rechecked in the jig.

A bend will be shown by a gap between the side of the piston and the jig.

Block

Before being used in a rebuild, the block must be checked for general condition. The casing should not be cracked, the deck should be flat or within tolerance for resurfacing, the cylinders must not be deeply scored and the main bearing caps or girdle must not have been subjected to a spun bearing (in which the bearing welds to the crankshaft and spins in the block, damaging the crankshaft bore).

With the connecting rods prepared, Deagle turns his attention to the engine block. The deck of the block must be checked for flatness: if it is untrue, it must be resurfaced. The deck of the RC engine is fine and will be left as-is. Shown in a wet mill, however, is a Civic 1200 block. Use of a lubricating mixture of water and water-soluable oil allows the wet mill to produce a much smoother surface than common dry processes.

If the block meets these general parameters, it must be thoroughly cleaned. There are several methods. Iron-blocked engines can be hot-tanked by an engine machine shop. This process will damage aluminum blocks, however. Aluminum blocks can be cleaned in large tanks of carburetor cleaner, in petroleum solvents, in water-based solvents or with soap and water. Whenever water is used, just be sure to blow all of it off the block and out of the oil galleries, and to spray light oil on any iron or steel parts such as the cylinder sleeves.

Kenny Deagle preaches meticulous cleaning, down to the cylinder head bolt holes which, on the third-generation Civic and CRX engines that RC builds many of, are often corroded. In the CRX engine he is working on, Deagle says: "A lot of corrosion and sludge has built up in the bolt holes. It will give a very false torque reading which will result in a blown head gasket almost immediately." Deagle cleans the bolt holes with a small brush and solvent. He says the corrosion's presence often makes itself known with a powerful smell when an engine is disassembled: "It smells really awful. You have to do it out in the open."

Once the block has been cleaned and inspected, the cylinders are honed, or bored and honed. Most Hondas can be bored as far as 0.040 in. oversize, but Honda generally supplies oversized pistons for just 0.020 and 0.010 in. overbores, and often only for the latter. When the block is honed, whether it has been bored or not, the process is slow and the measurement process exact.

Kenny Deagle starts with the pistons. In RC's engine, he is fitting forged, high-compression pistons that will be matched to a modified cylinder head, sidedraft carburetors, a header and high-performance exhaust system. The forged pistons "require an extra 0.0015 inch to 0.0020 inch of wall clearance," Deagle says. "So they sell what's called a hone-in piston—take your block and hone it to size; no boring's required. We'll do this with a four-blade Sunnen hone and make the liners straight to within 0.0002 inch." Deagle says this tolerance is much greater than he's observed from factory-fresh Honda engines whose cylinder bores he's seen vary as much as 0.0015 in.

Oscar Jackson and Kenny Deagle both advocate using Sunnen hones with rigidly located stones, rather than those with flexibly located stones. The rigid hones, they say, will straighten the cylinders, removing material where needed and leaving it where the diameter is sufficient. Deagle says the stones he uses are one step finer than those used by most engine machine shops.

He also uses a customized set of short stones for cases in which the middle of the cylinder is too narrow, but the tops and bottoms are all right. "They can concentrate on any area of the bore," Deagle says. "We keep the same stroke, without pulling it way high, and more or less achieve a perfectly straight liner." To confirm this, Deagle first measures the piston. He adds the necessary clearance, and transfers the resulting diameter to a dial bore gauge. "I'll measure the top, middle and bottom, and rotate it, so you get side to side, and you get the same thing." If the cylinder measures the same at all six points, within 0.0002 in., it's completed.

The block deck is measured for straightness and, for competition, is milled to the minimum height specification.

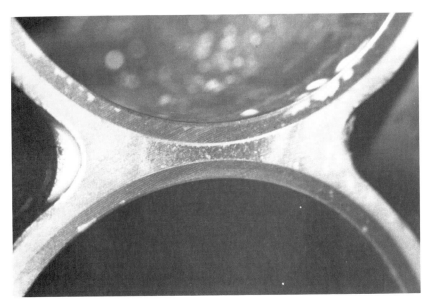

An initial pass of the mill shows a depression where a pair of cylinders are siamesed. Such a gap could allow a head gasket to blow, because the cylinder head would not clamp sufficiently at that spot.

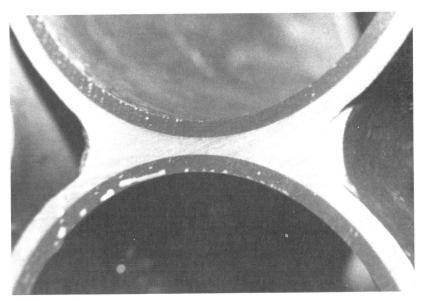

After removal of 0.004 in. of the deck, the depression disappears and the deck is usable again.

Once on the engine stand, Deagle inserts the main bearings and sprays engine-assembly oil in the main cap bolt holes.

The bolts and washers are lubricated as well to make sure the torque readings will be correct.

Before putting the CRX block on the engine stand, Deagle cleans it thoroughly with solvent in a parts washer. The holes for the cylinder head bolts and studs get close attention, he says: "A lot of corrosion and sludge has built up in the bolt holes. It will give a very false torque reading, which will result in a blown head gasket almost immediately. So this is critical, top and bottom. It will have a smell on it. It only appears to happen on these engines." The 1488 CRX engine is being rebuilt after 80,000 hard miles.

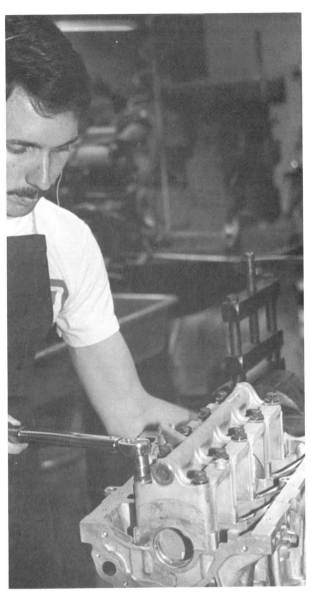

The crankshaft main cap girdle is bolted on with all main bearing shells in place. The bolts are torqued in a side-to-side, criss-cross pattern.

The crankshaft for this engine has already been balanced, but another Honda crank shows how it is fitted in the balancing machine.

Before being balanced, the counterweights of this engine's crankshaft were machined-down and knife-edged. The lighter weight improves throttle response and acceleration, while the knife-edging helps reduce resistance as the crankshaft rotates at high rpm through the cloud of engine oil and oil spray in the crankcase. A stock crankshaft is shown for comparison.

A close-up comparison of the race-prepped crank, left, with a stock crank.

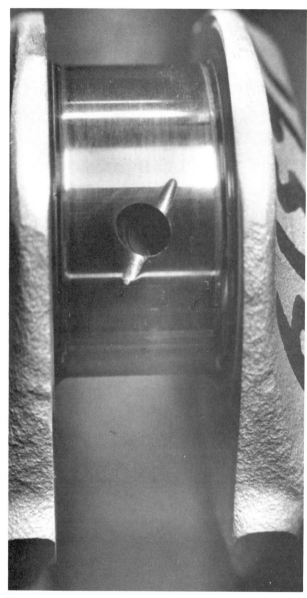

In a procedure much like that for the connecting rods and their bearings, the main journals of the crankshaft are measured with a micrometer.

The crankshaft's oil holes have also been chamfered to increase the flow of oil to the bearings.

The measurement is transferred to a dial bore gauge which measures the clearance of the corresponding main bearing.

The procedure must be repeated for each journal and main bearing to ensure that the clearances are those desired. The bearings are measured top to bottom, with Deagle shooting for a clearance of 0.0015 in.

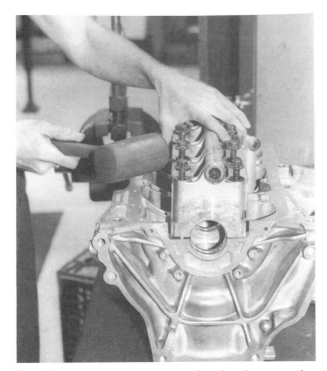

Once the measurements are completed and prove satisfactory, the girdle must be removed. The girdle fits tightly and can be stubborn to budge. A soft-faced rubber hammer or mallet should be used to rock it loose; never pry between the mating surfaces of the block and girdle because the resulting nick would destroy them.

Before installing the crankshaft, Deagle liberally coats the main bearings with assembly oil.

Then he carefully lowers the crankshaft into the block.

The thrust bearings limit forward and backward movement of the crankshaft. They are semi-circular when looked at from the side. Here, looked at from the bottom of the engine, only their ends can be seen along with the clearance between them and the crankshaft.

The thrust bearing clearance, called end play, is measured with a dial indicator on the end of the crankshaft. The crank is tapped in both directions with a mallet; the play for an engine like this should be 0.008 to 0.010 in., Deagle says.

uses a fine grade of glass bead to blast the top of the pistons, leaving smooth, rounded surfaces that are unlikely to produce hot spots and detonation. Two layers of wide masking tape protect the side of the piston during the bead blasting.

The piston rings are pressed squarely into their respective cylinders, one by one, and their gaps are measured. A stock piston, turned upside down, can be used to press the rings into the cylinders. "Then you just start feeding the rings on," Deagle says.

As he fits the rings to the pistons, Deagle watches for several potential problems: "It's extremely critical with the oil rings (in the bottom ring land) that the two ends butt up together and not overlap; you'd break the ends off." Noting that each level of ring should be spaced 120 degrees apart, Deagle says: "Go to your oil-scraper ring (the middle ring) and find the ID mark. What you do is rub an oily hand over it and you should be able to see it. It's critical that it's facing up." The same holds true for the top ring.

With the cylinders prepared, the rings installed on the pistons and the bearing shells in the rods and rod caps, use a ring compressor and the handle of a mallet or hammer to nudge the pistons into the cylinders. Have an assistant guide the connecting rods over the crankshaft so that the rod bolts do not gouge the crank throws; sliding a 2 in. section of fuel line over each rod bolt will help protect against gouging. As each rod is aligned with the crankshaft, the corresponding rod cap—in the proper orientation— is installed, and nuts are screwed onto the rod bolts and torqued down. Deagle advises against using Loctite or similar compounds on the bolts, and instead uses assembly oil or motor oil to lubricate the threads.

Both RC Engineering and Jackson Racing use a bolt-stretch gauge to measure the rod bolts' torque, in addition to a torque wrench. They feel that the amount of bolt stretch is the most accurate indicator. "That way," says Deagle, "if you have a bolt that feels spongy at 18 lb-ft, you can see what you're getting out of it."

Deagle also warns against over-tightening the rod bolts. "Some customers, we'll sell set-ups to and they assemble them. If they're used to working on domestic engines and they see 20 lb-ft, it just doesn't jive. I had one guy go out and torque them to 35 lb-ft, and he didn't finish the race."

With the proper end play confirmed, the main bearing girdle is bolted in again and retorqued. No thread-locking compound like Loctite is used on these bolts, Deagle says, as it can cause a false torque reading.

Pistons and rings

The forged pistons for RC's engine could be installed just as they come from the factory, says Kenny Deagle. But to ward off detonation, he uses a machinist's deburring tool to blunt the sharp edges around the valve reliefs in the piston domes. Then he

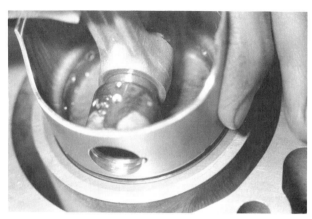

Now that the crankshaft has been installed, the engine is turned over and Kenny focuses his attention on the cylinders. They have been honed with a four-blade rigid hone and are ready for checking the piston ring gaps; each ring must be checked in its respective cylinder.

Then an upside-down piston is used to press the ring part way down the cylinder.

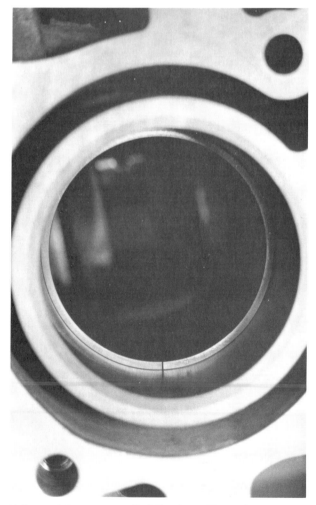

A feeler gauge is used to measure the gap between the ends of the ring; the gap must fall within the specifications.

Using a piston ensures that the ring will remain square in the bore.

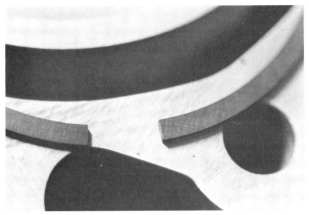

The identification marks on these rings, when the rings are installed on the pistons, must face up.

RC Engineering's engine will use forged high-compression pistons, supplied by A-T Engineering. To keep hot spots from forming on the piston tops, Deagle first uses a machinist's deburring tool to blunt sharp edges and corners. Then he prepares the piston for bead blasting by masking all except the top.

In a bead blasting cabinet, Deagle focuses on the piston tops. A bead blaster is similar to a sand blaster, but is not as abrasive.

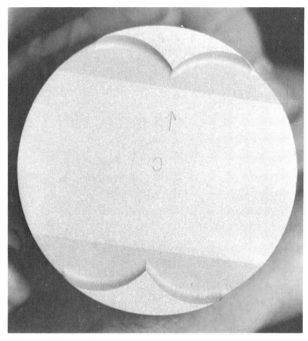

The result is a slightly coarse surface with rounded, flowing edges around the valve reliefs.

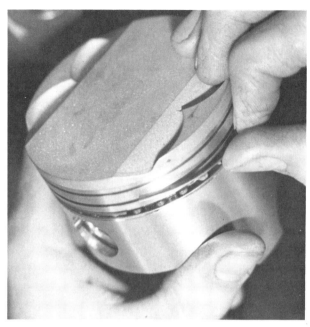

Deagle feeds the middle and upper rings onto the pistons one-by-one. Once a piston has the oil rings, the middle ring and the top ring installed, Deagle aligns them at 120 degree intervals so the gaps do not overlap.

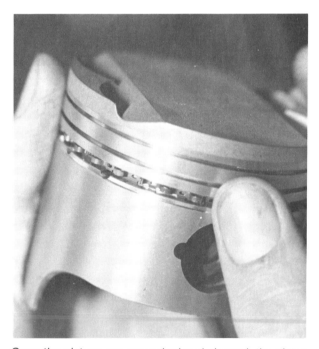

Once the pistons are unmasked and cleaned, the piston rings are installed. Deagle installs them by hand, careful to avoid breaking a ring. He starts with the oil rings. Deagle warns to install the oil rings exactly as specified: "It's extremely critical with the oil rings that the two end butt up together and not overlap. You'd break the ends off."

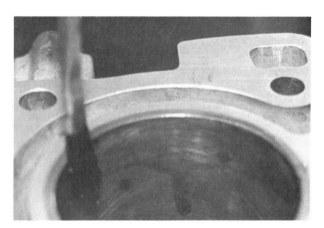

Before the pistons are installed, Deagle coats the cylinders with assembly oil.

Using a piston ring compressor on the piston, Deagle taps the piston top with the handle of a hammer to slide it into the cylinder.

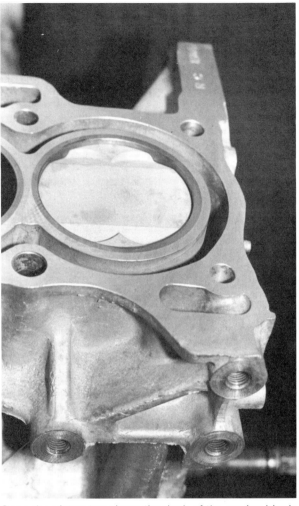

Once the piston top clears the deck of the engine block, the compressor is removed. The work then moves to the bottom of the engine, at the crankshaft journal.

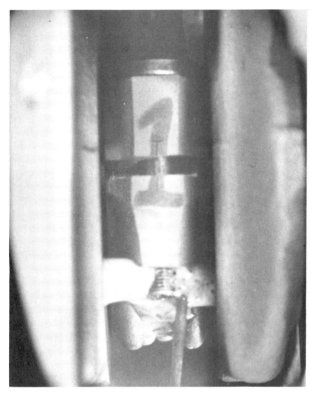

The connecting rod cap is installed with its bearing insert, and the rod bolt is coated with assembly oil.

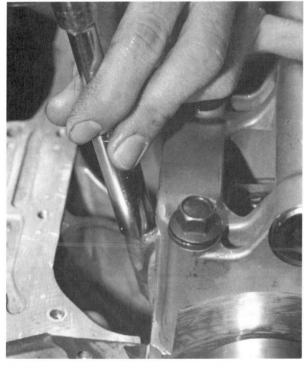

The bolts are tightened. Again, bolt stretch will govern the nut's tightness rather than torque applied against the nut.

As with the other parts, the cleaning of the oil pump is thorough. The gasket surface gets a wire brush scrubbing to ensure a good seal.

The interior of the pump is gone over with a brush. The oil supply must be perfectly clean at the first start-up.

The best sealing compound for front-mounted Honda oil pumps, Deagle says, is the Honda semi-drying gasket which comes in a tube.

The oil pump is then mounted in place.

Once the dowels are placed in the housing, it may be bolted onto the block.

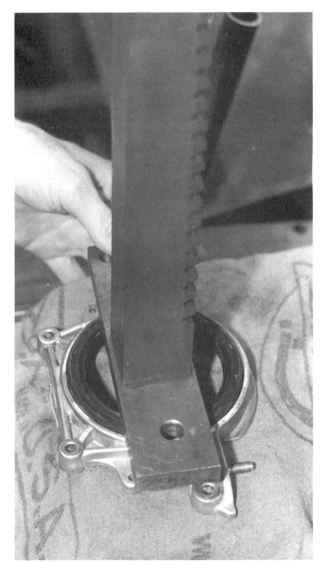

An arbor press is used to install the rear main oil seal in its housing. The seal must fit squarely.

Loctite thread-locking compound is used on the oil pump pickup tube to keep its nuts from vibrating loose and starving the engine for oil.

The oil pump pickup tube is then bolted into place.

Only a few items remain before the short block—the engine minus the cylinder head—is completed. Installing the cylinder head studs is one of those last steps.

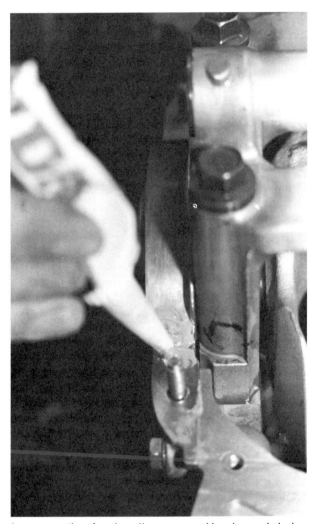
In preparation for the oil pan, more Honda semi-drying gasket is used at the corners of the engine. Deagle is a believer in the compound, saying, "It doesn't set up. It's real nice stuff." He prefers it to silicone sealers, saying that it is better at preventing oil leaks and noting that it comes off easily with light scraping.

Next is the installation of the water pump.

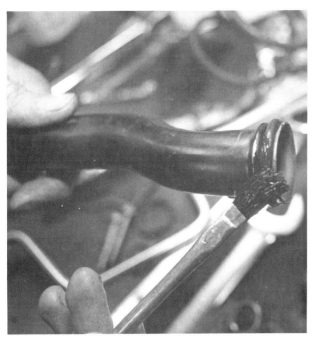

With the addition of the thermostat housing and crankcase breather, the short block is completed.

Installation of the water pump inlet tube is made easier with a bit of oil on the outside of the O-ring. Coating the whole O-ring will make it roll off the tube, however, Deagle says.

Before the engine is installed, a lightened flywheel, right, will be fitted. The flywheel is produced from a stock flywheel, left, that is machined down in a lathe.

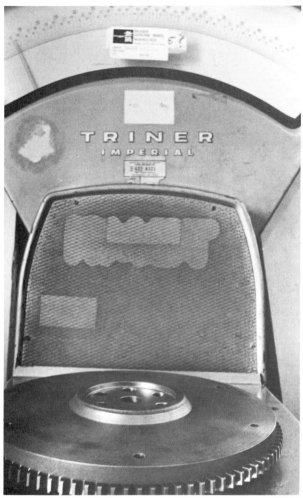

The purpose of the lightened flywheel is partially the same as for the lightened crankshaft: to increase throttle response and acceleration. The machined flywheel is about three pounds lighter than the stock version, and is not intended for street use.

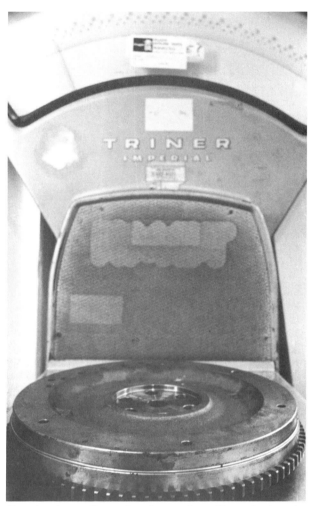

For street use, the pulse-dampening effect of a heavier flywheel should be relatively smooth idling.

RC recommends heat-treated valve spring retainers. After extended high-rpm use, the stock retainers can pull past the conical split valve keepers, dropping its valve.

The result of a failed valve spring retainer and dropped valve in one engine was this destroyed piston.

Cylinder head

If there's something that nearly all builders of high-performance engines agree on, it's that the cylinder head holds the greatest potential for power improvement. In absolutely stock engines, the only variance can be in the width and location of the seating areas machined on the valves and valve seats. Each builder develops specifications he believes to produce the greatest airflow and surest sealing, and therefore the greatest power. Because of this, the exact specifications are closely guarded secrets. But generally, valve jobs are done with cuts machined at 30 degrees, 45 degrees (the face on which the valve seats) and 60 degrees. And the machinists try to remove as little material as possible when machining the valves and valve seats to keep from sinking the valve and reducing airflow.

For RC's 1984 engine, the cylinder head is replaced with an Si head without the CVCC pre-chambers. With modified engines such as RC's, mild

porting is called for. On twelve-valve Civic/CRX engines such as this, a small ridge is cast into the port just under the valve seat. Grinding the ridge away is the first step Tom Deagle undertakes. "That really improves the flow on these heads," he says. Additionally, Deagle unshrouds the valves by grinding small reliefs in the combustion chambers next to the valve seats. In the chambers for the RC engine, Deagle says, "there's a shroud going around that we blend in. Another thing we do is smooth everything out where it was rough from the factory. We bead blast them, which leaves a nice surface."

Tom Deagle also bead blasts the valve heads, after taping the stems for protection, to clean them in preparation for refacing. This work is done on a valve refacing machine that rotates the valve while a motor-driven grinding wheel contacts its faces lightly. The wheel can be set at different angles to grind the required faces. "I give it about two strokes" on the 45 degree face, Deagle says. It generally takes off about 0.0005 in. "Then what we do to make it really trick," he says, "is reposition the grinder to 30 degrees, and it will cut a 30."

Deagle uses heat-treated valve spring retainers to keep the valves from pulling out of their retainers after extended high-rpm use. The valve guides are checked for wear; on RC's engine, they are in good condition. For heads needing new guides, the procedure is to heat the cylinder head on a hot plate for about two hours, until it reaches 500 degrees. At that point the head has expanded sufficiently to press the guides out. "Once it's hot enough," Deagle says, "the guides slide right out." The head remains hot to receive the new guides, which have been cooled so they will contract. "They should just slide right in with light tapping."

The valve seats must be cut with the same precision as the valve faces; 30, 45 and 60 degree angles are ground on the seats. "I like to start with the 60," says Deagle, "go with the 30 and finish with the 45 because I have a feel for these heads—where to stop everything. But the ideal way to do it is just about the opposite: Start off with the 45, and true it up with the 60 and 30 to get the exact angle." Deagle stresses that the 45 degree cut is the most important. "The 45 is what makes the seal. If it's not completely at the same angle as the valve, you're not going to get a good seal." For this reason, he says, the stones used for grinding must be trued carefully and the valve-grinding machine must be exactly calibrated.

Once the valves and seats are ground, each valve is lapped by hand into its seat with lapping compound, an abrasive paste that removes any high spots. The compound is spread on the valve face, and the

93

valve then is rotated in the seat until the compound etches an even pattern on the 45 degree faces. Tom Deagle numbers each valve with a felt marker as he goes along to make sure there is no confusion in final assembly. "I number everything—way more than most people do." He says that, besides avoiding confusion with work that spans more than a day, another worker can pick up the pieces and complete the job if he is out.

As with the block, RC Engineering decks its cylinder heads to the minimum thickness specified by Honda or by an amount requested by the customer. "That bumps the compression ratio," Deagle says, adding that it can also throw off the valve timing. An adjustable camshaft chain sprocket is used to compensate in extreme cases.

"The head is the most important part. You can have a very lousy bottom end, but put a new head on it and it will run perfectly—it will run great so long as you don't have any broken rings or anything like that. That's why they can be so expensive to get from the right people," Deagle says.

Oscar Jackson agrees, saying "The head is what really makes the thing fly."

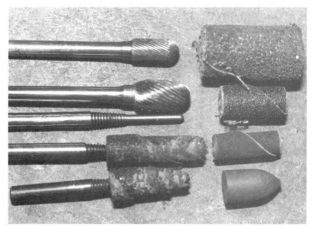
For porting cylinder heads, Tom Deagle uses various grinding bits and abrasive rolls.

Tom attaches the cylinder head to a special ball-jointed mount that allows him to swivel the head over a wide range of positions.

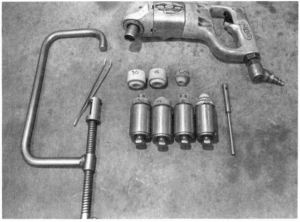
Kenny Deagle's brother Tom is RC Engineering's cylinder head specialist. Among his tools are, from left, a valve spring compressor, tweezers, an air-powered valve seat grinder, and mandrels and stones for grinding the valves.

With the retainer loose, Deagle uses tweezers to remove the split valve keepers. He prefers them to the magnets and needle-nosed pliers often used by others. He finds the tweezers quicker and more accurate.

The C-clamp style valve spring compressor exerts pressure on the valve head from below and on the valve spring retainer from above. As it is tightened down, pressure on the retainer is relaxed.

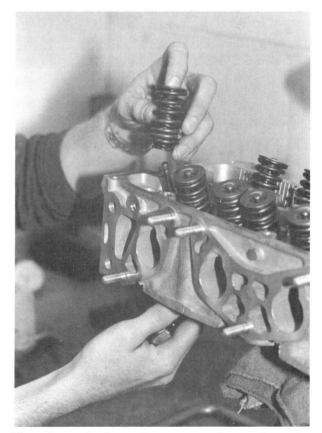

The valve and valve springs are now free, and may be removed.

A used valve, right, will be carbon-encrusted.

The cleaned valve, right, will look much like the ground and lapped valve, left, except for its face.

Deagle takes the valve to the bead blasting cabinet for cleaning.

For refacing, the valve is placed in a grinder and aligned. Once aligned at the main angle of 45 degrees, the motor is turned on, the grinding wheel is brought up to the valve and the least amount of material possible is removed to true the valve face around its circumference. Once the valve and wheel are "barely touching, then I give it about two strokes," Deagle says. "It generally takes off about 0.0005 in. Then what we do to make it really trick is reposition it and cut it 30 degrees."

In a similar way, a minimum of material is ground from the valve seats.

The valves and seats mate on their 45 degree angles, and it is there where they are lapped with valve grinding compound to complete the valve job. The stripe across the face of the valve shows where the seat was lapped into the valve.

Three stones are used: a 30 degree stone, a 45 and a 60. This is the 45.

For improving the intake and exhaust ports, Deagle suggests first smoothing over these ridges.

The cylinder head's intake and exhaust ports have been massaged with careful grinding and polishing. This is the intake side.

The completed 1488 CRX Si cylinder head is ready for installation on the short block. Its combustion chambers have been smoothed by bead blasting.

The interior of the cylinder head is spotlessly clean, as is the rest of the engine.

6

Producing more power

If the game plan for your car includes greater power, the plan should also spell out how dramatic the increase will be. Changes that amount to fine-tuning the engine—say, through improvements in carburetion, exhaust or ignition components—are compatible with a stock engine in good condition. More substantial alterations like high-compression pis-

tons, radically reground camshafts or high-boost turbocharging may require a racing-type engine rebuild.

Not only is it important from a durability standpoint to know what to expect from each piece of equipment added to the engine or substituted for a factory part, it's vital to choose components that are

Nitrous oxide systems, such as that installed on this Civic CVCC engine, can provide short bursts of extremely high power. They do so by injecting nitrous oxide and additional gasoline into the engine, increasing the amount of fuel and oxygen in the combustion chamber (derived from the nitrous oxide). The nitrous oxide gas is compressed in a high-pressure bottle; its flow is controlled by switch-operated solenoids mounted on the firewall. This engine is

from the Modified class ice racer built by OHV Motors of Eden Prairie, Minnesota, and run in the 1989 season by driver P. D. Cunningham. The engine is carbureted by dual sidedraft Webers, and all fuel and oil is routed through Russell stainless steel fasteners and hoses. The car is further modified with a partial tube frame and a Jackson Racing rear wing. *Tim Parker*

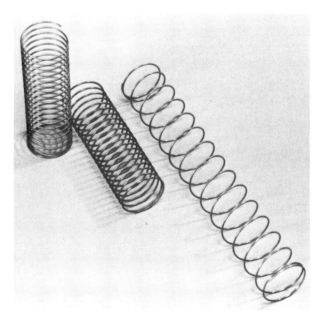

These specially wound springs are sold by Jackson Racing for the Prelude constant-velocity carburetors. They allow the carburetor pistons to open quicker, improving throttle response and acceleration. *Jackson Racing*

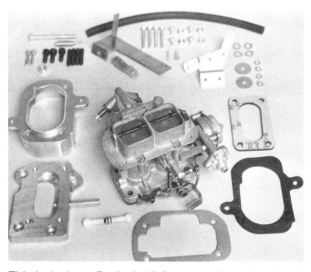

This is Jackson Racing's kit for converting a two-barrel Weber 32–36 mm DGEV downdraft carburetor to the 1488 CVCC engine. The carb is pre-jetted, and the kit includes aluminum manifold-to-carburetor adapter and mounting hardware. *Jackson Racing*

compatible with one another. Otherwise, the expected power increase may not result. For instance, using a camshaft intended for high rpm in an otherwise unaltered engine could result in less low-rpm output than stock, and choked-off performance at high rpm. Such a camshaft would require high-flow carburetion and exhaust systems, and quite likely increased compression, to show its potential.

When considering these changes, keep in mind the four-stroke combustion cycle that all Honda auto engines, including the CVCC models, use. The cycle goes as follows:

1. The downward intake stroke of the piston sucks air and fuel into the cylinder.

2. The upward compression stroke squeezes the fuel-air mixture between the piston top and combustion chamber.

3. The ignition fires just as the piston is reaching the top of the cylinder and the mixture is at full compression. That's when the burning mixture can produce the greatest amount of power. The downward power stroke is produced by the rapid expansion of the burning fuel-air mixture.

4. The upward exhaust stroke forces the burned mixture from the cylinder.

Each of the following modifications, from carburetor to flywheel, helps the engine make better use of the four-stroke cycle.

Carburetion

Four types of carburetion are found on Hondas: two-barrel downdraft carburetor, three-barrel downdraft carburetor, twin sidedraft constant-velocity carburetors and PGM-FI fuel injection. Each one can be improved upon with stock engines.

Different carburetion is a must for high-rpm use. Keep in mind, however, that these performance improvements may be illegal in your area for emission-control reasons or may not be allowed in certain racing classes. Depending on your situation, read the applicable laws and rules before moving ahead.

Because manufacturers like Honda must tune their carburetors for the best compromise between emissions, fuel economy and power, some gain in power and driveability can be found through recalibration. Kits with replacement carburetor jets are available for some models, or in the case of the Prelude's sidedraft carburetors, replacement springs for the constant-velocity pistons can be bought. Drills for enriching carburetor jets by increasing the diameter of their orifices also are sold. The purpose of these changes is to allow the carburetors to produce a richer fuel-air mixture which in turn will result

A single Weber 40 DCOE two-barrel sidedraft carburetor on a Canon manifold was used by George E. Cleveland of Birmingham, Alabama, during 1988 on his 1977 Civic 1200 autocross car. Cleveland competes in D Street Prepared.

For 1989 he installed a pair of 40 mm SK carburetors (not shown) but says he found little performance difference between the two set-ups with his internally stock 1237 engine.

in greater power. Exhaust emissions and fuel economy will generally suffer, however.

Replacement carburetors that can be adapted to the stock intake manifold are the next step. A wide array of downdraft carburetors for Hondas is offered by different tuners and carburetor distributors. Most are based on the Weber DGV series of two-barrel carburetors. This carburetor line—whose models are available with various throttle-bore sizes, and manual and automatic chokes—is known for its quick throttle response and good driveability. Also, most DGV carburetors have larger barrels and venturis than the carburetors installed by Honda. This allows the engine to produce greater power at higher rpm because the larger carburetor openings permit greater airflow.

Also popular, both with relatively stock engines and high-rpm engines, are replacement sidedraft carburetor kits. These sidedraft carburetors are unlike those used on the Prelude. Instead, they usually consist of twin two-barrel carburetors—one barrel per cylinder—either made by Weber or patterned after the long-popular Weber racing carburetor. Other manufacturers include Dell'Orto, Mikuni, SK and Solex. They are distributed by a wide variety of companies, and packaged with several different manifolds and throttle-linkage kits. Generally, however, they use 40 mm size carburetors; a 35 mm kit is sold for the Civic 1200 and kits with single sidedraft Weber carburetors are also sold.

This Weber 32 DGV downdraft carburetor replaces the original Hitachi downdraft on a stock 1237 and is used for Improved Touring competition on the author's 1974 Civic.

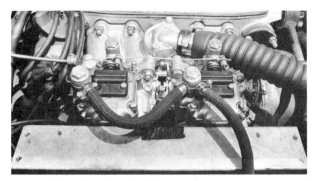

This A-T Engineering Dell'Orto carburetor set-up is used on the author's Civic, when it competes in the SCCA's D Street Prepared autocross class. The dual sidedraft carburetors have 35 mm throttles and look like miniature Webers. The compact package will just squeeze between the stock distributor and fuel pump. It lowers 0–60 mph time by about one second from the Weber 32 DGV also used on the car.

Roberson's D Prepared autocrossing Civic uses twin Weber 40 DCOE sidedraft carburetors—a tight fit.

Twin two-barrel carburetion on a four-cylinder engine holds the advantage over other carburetor arrangements because each barrel feeds directly into its corresponding intake port. There's no convoluted manifold passages to disrupt flow or disturb the fuel-air mixture as there are with single-carburetor systems. The twin-carb setups are compatible with stock-type and high-rpm racing engines because of their extreme adjustability. Most importantly, a variety of venturi sizes is available. Smaller venturis keep the airflow up at lower speeds, mixing fuel and air evenly, providing good driveability and throttle response. At the same time, the direct manifolding provides high-speed power improvements. Larger venturis are used with high-rpm engines in which low-speed response and driveability are not critical, but minimum airflow restriction is. The large venturis allow maximum airflow for maximum power output.

Tuning these carburetors can be time-consuming. In fact, books have been written just on the subject of tuning the Weber sidedraft. So it's best to work with your supplier to find a carburetor setup that's tuned to an engine combination like yours. This is one advantage of sticking to a single company when chosing carburetors, camshafts, exhaust and so on, because these suppliers generally tune the carburetors in combination with the other components they sell.

CVCC engines can use these replacement carburetors as well. Downdraft carburetor kits that adapt to stock manifolds and sidedraft multi-carb rigs that include their own manifolds are sold and work well. They do defeat the purpose of the CVCC

The 1488 Si engine of Grady Wood's CRX uses dual 40 mm Webers as well. Wood works closely with Chuck Noonan, whose Chuck's Civic Center tuning shop has been renamed CRE/Performance.

Bob Endicott's RC Engineering-built 1488 Si differs externally from Wood's largely in using Mikuni carburetors rather than Webers. Endicott also used air filters versus Wood's velocity stacks.

This stock 1989 Civic Si engine uses Honda's PGM-FI electronic port fuel injection system. The system is compact and neat.

With dual 40 DCOE Webers or similar large carburetion set-ups on the Civic 1200 engine, an A-T Engineering angled distributor drive is needed to clear the sidedraft bodies, like this example on Angelo Roberson's car.

system, however. CVCC engines use a small third carburetor barrel to feed each cylinder's pre-chamber with a rich fuel-air mixture. The main carburetor circuits feed the combustion chamber with lean fuel-air mixture.

The adaptors or intake manifolds for replacement CVCC carburetors are rigged to feed the main intake ports and the CVCC intake ports with the same fuel-air mixture. While the pre-chamber mixture is leaner than with a Honda carburetor, it still is within the range that can be ignited by a spark plug. The rest of the process—flame ignition of the main combustion chamber—takes place in the normal CVCC manner. However, the low exhaust emissions and high fuel mileage attributed to the standard CVCC system are lost because the combustion process becomes essentially the same as in a non-CVCC engine, even though combustion still starts in the pre-chamber rather than the main chamber.

With fuel-injected Hondas there are few ways to modify the system. Luckily, few changes are needed

because the accuracy of electronic fuel injection allows Honda to make fewer compromises between performance, fuel economy and emissions. Tweaks can be made on a case-by-case basis by electronics or carburetion experts, but few parts are sold for this purpose. With a stock engine, a slight power increase may be found by switching to two sidedraft carburetors, although driveability and fuel economy will be reduced somewhat. For modified engines, the adjustability of the sidedrafts make them the choice over fuel injection although, with enough high-tech tinkering, the fuel injection might prove superior.

Turbochargers

Designers of turbocharging systems have the same end result in mind as those who design free-flowing carburetors and intake manifolds: to get a greater volume of fuel and air into the engine. The means are completely different, however. Rather than just optimizing intake passages, turbo systems use an air pump—the turbocharger—to force more fuel and air into the engine.

For the record, any air pump used for this purpose is a supercharger. Superchargers traditionally were driven by belts or gears connected to the crankshaft. The more recently developed turbocharger is a particular type of supercharger that is driven by a small turbine (a wheel with thin vanes that looks like a multi-bladed propellor). The turbine is inserted in the exhaust system. Exhaust flow propels the turbine which is connected to a shaft that drives a second turbine. This second turbine is inserted in the intake system and pumps air—or a fuel-air mixture, depending on its location in the system—into the engine.

The more power the engine makes, the greater the exhaust flow, and the greater the exhaust, the

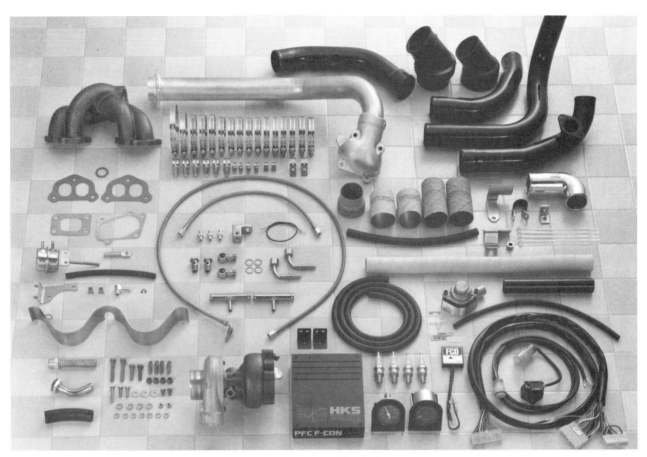

These components make up the HKS Stage 1 turbocharging system for the third-generation CRX Si and Civic Si. It works with the Honda fuel injection system and produces 4 psi of boost, which HKS says results in 120 hp at 5000 rpm. *HKS USA Inc.*

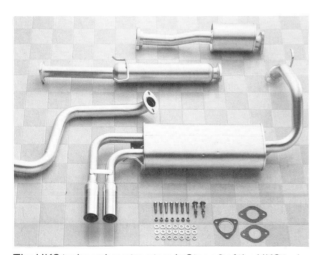

The HKS turbo exhaust system is Stage 2 of the HKS turbo kit. The California company, which is Japan-based, says the system adds 0.5 psi of boost to the turbo kit and raises power to 135 hp at 5000 rpm. *HKS USA Inc.*

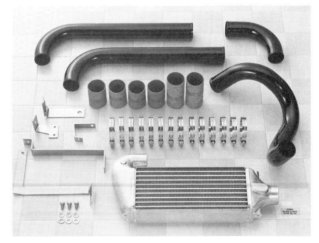

Stage 3 of the HKS turbo kit consists of four parts. The first is this air-to-air intercooler, used to lower the temperature of the air entering the engine. *HKS USA Inc.*

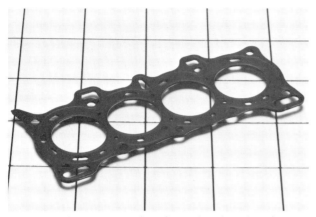

The second component is a 2 mm head gasket that reduces the compression ratio from 8.7:1 to 8.0:1, decreasing the possibility of combustion chamber detonation. *HKS USA Inc.*

HKS's variable boost control allows the boost to be adjusted between 4 psi and 12 psi, and is the third component. *HKS USA Inc.*

greater the air pumping. This pumping is known as boost because once the turbo is running at high speed it pumps more air than the engine can use, boosting the intake manifold pressure above atmospheric pressure. The greater the boost, the greater the power, the greater the exhaust and, again, the greater the boost. Followed to its logical end this cycle would continue until the engine exploded or burned up. In fact this, in simple terms, is the ultimate problem facing turbocharger designers.

The problem in greater detail is that forcing too much fuel and air, or allowing the mixture to overheat, into the engine results in detonation—early, uncontrollable explosion of the fuel and air because of high temperature or pressure, rather than even burning of the mixture. This in turn can melt piston tops, burn valves or blow the head gasket, or cause other parts to fail. Control problems of this sort were the downfall of many turbo systems in the 1970s when they first gained popularity as add-on kits. With the wide availability of microprocessors and electronic fuel injection systems in the 1980s, most systems gained more exact controls. For instance, with these second-generation turbo systems, an engine control computer can retard the ignition timing at the advent of detonation or reduce the boost, or do both to eliminate detonation. Once the detonation subsides, the computer can add more ignition advance or boost, keeping the engine just below the danger point.

Water-cooled turbo bearings

Because the turbocharger turns in the range of 100,000 rpm, precise bearings are used which need a constant, clean and cool supply of oil. This is complicated by the turbo's connection to the exhaust system

whose temperature exceeds 1,000 degrees Fahrenheit; most engine oil begins breaking down as it reaches 300 degrees. By casting a water jacket around the bearings and passing engine coolant through it, turbo manufacturers have managed to cool the oil as it lubricates the bearings, greatly increasing their life.

High-flow fuel injectors and a special computer chip round out HKS's Stage 3 kit, and show the kind of specialization required to produce a proper turbocharging system. *HKS USA Inc.*

Turbo timers

Even with water-cooled bearings, oil around the bearings can become overheated under certain conditions. Usually this happens when the car is driven hard, bringing the exhaust and turbo up to top temperature. Damage can result if the engine then is turned off without a cooling-down period. Since the coolant stops flowing through the turbo's water jacket, the oil can overheat. When the heat is so severe that the oil not only breaks down but solidifies, the bearings are ruined. This process is called coking.

A turbo timer can solve this problem by allowing the engine to continue idling when the key is turned off. The engine runs long enough to cool the turbo and then the timer turns off the engine. Even if the turbo isn't water-cooled, the extended pumping of oil through the turbo at idle will fight coking. It's eerie to turn off the car, remove the key and leave with the engine still running, but a turbo timer is a simple and effective way to increase the longevity of a turbocharger.

Do *not* use a turbo timer in a closed garage, however, because of the poisonous carbon monoxide that would build up.

Better oil

While developments in oil aren't changes in the turbo systems themselves, they have allowed improvements. Since turbo kits became common in the 1970s, the top rating for engine oil has been raised several times. The ability to stand up to higher temperatures has been one of the most important factors in these tougher oil standards. With this greater heat resistance, the better oils fight coking and extend the longevity of turbo bearings.

When buying oil for any Honda, but particularly one with a turbo kit, pick one that meets the highest standard. And consider a synthetic oil. Some synthetic oils have an extraordinary ability to withstand high temperature. In choosing one, make sure the oil meets the top US standard. Also buy a brand-name synthetic, or one that a Honda specialist or turbo company you're dealing with has tested thoroughly; ask their advice.

There is a variety of opinions on preventing coking. Corky Bell of Cartech Inc., which manufactures turbo systems for the 1985–87 CRX Si and the 1988–89 CRX Si, as well as for other makes and models, says that frequent oil changing is the most certain way to avoid the problem. Coking develops as the oil—depleted of its high-temperature additives through overuse—passes through the turbocharger's bearings over a relatively long period, rather than after shutdown, Bell says. Oil changes every 2,500 to 3,000 miles will prevent coking without using exotic oils, turbo timers or water-cooled bearings, he says, although nearly all of Cartech's systems employ water-cooled turbos.

The greater problem for durability, Bell says, is maintaining the correct fuel-air ratio. "You've got to have a good air-fuel ratio, or you don't have a properly functioning—and probably not even a safe—turbo system." An additional consideration, relatively unrelated to durability but critical for good performance is a properly sized turbocharger, he says. "The size is two things: it is the turbine and the compressor," says Bell about the exhaust and intake sections of the turbo. "You need to have the turbine drive the compressor fast enough to make a reasonable amount of boost at low end and mid range, yet when you get to the top end you cause an excess of backpressure between the turbine and the combustion chamber. You want to reduce that backpressure to the least-possible amount, and get good low-end response and good mid-range torque."

The result of an oversized turbo is substantial lag between the time the accelerator boost is produced; the engine will be particularly sluggish at low speeds. An undersized turbocharger, on the other hand, will have sharp throttle response but will not increase maximum power greatly. Bell says the compromise between response and power depends on the designer's goals, but adds that generally the turbocharger should be at its peak efficiency at the engine speed that it will most often be used. For most street engines, that's at the speed at which it makes its greatest torque. For racing engines, that will be closer to the speed at which the engine makes its greatest horsepower.

If you consider buying a turbo system, think about the rpm range you'll be using the engine in most, and then find out what range the systems you're considering works in. Finally, before buying and installing a turbo system, try to locate someone who is using the system you're considering, and asking their opinion of it; drive the car if possible.

Intercoolers

When air is pressurized, it heats up. That's a fact of physics that fights the quest for power through turbocharging, or any kind of supercharging for that matter. The greater the heat, the sooner the power limit from detonation will be reached. With a turbocharger, the heating is compounded by the turbo's connection to the exhaust system which transfers more heat to the air being pumped into the engine.

An intercooler is like a radiator for the intake system. Placed between the turbo and the intake manifold, it cools the air as it enters the engine. With most intercoolers, the intake air is piped to the intercooler which contains passageways that are finned on the outside. As the intake air moves through the passages, it transfers the heat to the fins.

The intercooler usually is mounted at the front of the car. The moving car's airstream cools the fins, finally taking away the heat that originated with the turbocharger. The cooled air then is piped back into the intake manifold. A less common design passes the intake air through a cooler containing water jackets. The air passes its heat into the water jackets; the water is piped to a radiator separate from the engine's radiator. The airflow at the front of the car cools the water which is pumped back to the intercooler. The intake air is piped from the intercooler into the intake manifold.

If you consider a turbo system to work with a fuel-injected engine (a second-generation system), look for one that the manufacturer guarantees to be compatible with a stock engine. If you consider a turbo system that uses a carburetor, also look for one compatible with a stock engine and one that uses relatively low boost—say, in the range of five to seven pounds per square inch.

Pistons

Pistons can increase power three ways. The first is by being lighter and raising the rpm limit. The second is by raising the compression ratio to pack the fuel and air more tightly into the combustion chamber. (The compression ratio is calculated by taking the volume of the cylinder and combustion chamber when the piston is at the bottom of the cylinder, and dividing it by the volume when the piston is at the top of the cylinder. In the case of a 9:1 compression ratio, the piston squeezes the fuel-air mixture during its upward stroke to one-ninth its original volume.) The third method is by lowering the compression ratio when used in conjunction with a turbocharging system and thus allowing higher boost levels without detonation.

The first approach is one that makes good theoretical sense and would be taken into consideration in building a racing engine. For Honda enthusiasts who aren't looking to change compression ratio, the stock pistons are fine. Honda is known for its lightweight, high-strength engine components and there's little to be gained here except in an all-out racing engine.

The second and third approaches seem contradictory but are not as their aims are the same: to create a denser fuel-air mixture for the spark plug to fire. The denser this mixture is, the more molecules of fuel and air that can be packed into each cubic centimeter of the combustion chamber. This density

Mugen was founded by Hirotoshi Honda, the son of Soichiro Honda, to make motocross performance parts as bolt-on equipment for Honda motorcycles; over the years, Mugen developed Honda automobile performance parts. These are Mugen forged pistons for 1986–89 Integras. A single piston ring is used for low drag and the piston pin bosses are reinforced to cope with the long stroke of the Integra engine when used for performance applications. King Motorsports of Milwaukee is the American Mugen distributor. *King Motorsports*

is the key to greater power, whether achieved by removing restrictions in the intake or exhaust systems, by raising the compression ratio or by pumping more air and fuel into the engine. That's because a denser fuel-air mixture will produce more heat. And more heat translates into greater power—an engine is a heat-to-power converter.

In the case of a naturally aspirated engine—one that is not supercharged—raising the compression ratio raises the mixture's density, making it burn hotter. Like a turbocharger boost, compression can be raised too much and cause detonation. The consequences are just as destructive as too much boost.

In the case of a turbocharged engine, lowering the compression ratio may allow the turbo system to pump more air and fuel into the engine before detonation occurs. In this case, the mixture density is raised by forcing in more fuel and air molecules. Even though the ratio of compression is lower, the density increases because the mixture enters the engine under high pressure; less additional pressurization through compression is required.

Ignition system

Except for early Hondas that used breaker-point ignition systems, the Honda electronic ignition systems are high quality and are fine for high-performance use on most naturally aspirated street engines.

The King Motorsports tube-frame CRX GT3 racer uses Mugen electronic ignition to spark its 210 horsepower engine. The car uses four separate coils to fire each of the four cylinders. *G. William Krause*

Racing engines or turbocharged street engines may require stronger ignition. The denser fuel-air mixtures they produce are the reason: they're more difficult to fire by spark.

If you're installing a turbo kit, follow the kit manufacturer's recommendation for ignition. Otherwise, there's a vast array of electronic ignition systems that are suitable for racing. Most provide their improvements by raising the voltage and current that reaches the spark plug. A few multiple-spark systems reduce misfiring by charging each spark plug several times in rapid succession on the power stroke.

Check with the company supplying your other racing parts to see what it has tested and found to be the best. Chances are, that company's had a greater opportunity to experiment with components than you have and has found a system that works well with your combination of components.

Exhaust system

Like the intake system, clearing the exhaust system of obstructions can bring a gain in power. Doing so opens a freer pathway for burned fuel and air exiting the engine. Unlike similar intake-system modifications, this does not necessarily result in more fuel and air being drawn into the engine. The first priority of a high-performance exhaust system is to reduce backpressure. The exhaust is hot and expanding as it exits the engine, and at high speed it pressurizes the system; this pressure is called backpressure. Reducing backpressure allows the engine to purge the cylinder of more exhaust gas before the

piston begins the intake stroke. Doing so is important because a fuel-air mixture diluted by remnant exhaust gas will burn cooler and produce less power. It's like having an extra exhaust-gas-recirculation system for emissions control.

A good exhaust system can perform several other functions, including pulse tuning and power-band shifting, although to a lesser degree on a street car than a race car.

Pulse tuning

Every time an exhaust valve opens, particularly when the engine is running at high speed, a strong pulse of exhaust shoots out the exhaust port into the exhaust manifold. This pulse can also be considered a column of exhaust gas with a given diameter, length and speed at a particular rpm and throttle opening.

By grouping the exhaust manifold passage for each of the four cylinders together a certain distance from the cylinder head, the manifold can be arranged so that the passage of one column of exhaust creates a suction in the passage for the cylinder that begins the exhaust stroke next. This suction helps pull the exhaust from the next cylinder; it lessens backpressure. The effect is like that from standing on a roadside when a large truck speeds by. The suction from the passing truck, the equivalent of a column of exhaust, pulls us toward the back of the truck.

A well-designed header is needed to make use of this phenomenon. A header is an exhaust manifold made from tubular steel. While factory manifolds are cast, headers are welded from tubing because they're lighter, easier to make in small and moderate quantities, and because it's easier to make small changes for experimentation.

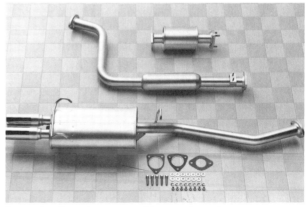

A good exhaust system, with no other changes, can add power to a Honda. HKS claims an 11 hp increase from this system, which fits late 1985 through 1987 Preludes. *HKS USA Inc.*

Powerband shifting

The tuning of exhaust pulses generally brings power increases to just a limited rpm range. Because engines produce different amounts of power over the full range of rpm, tuners section the overall range into segments called powerbands. Header manufacturers alter the lengths and diameters of the pipes, and sometimes their configuration to meet their powerband goals. There are two common header configurations: tri-Y and four-into-one.

Tri-Y headers pair the tubes from cylinders 1 and 4, and cylinders 2 and 3 about halfway down the manifold. This leaves two larger tubes that run the rest of the header's length and join one another underneath the car where the header connects to the rest of the exhaust system. This configuration generally is used to boost low-speed power. An engine with strength in this lower powerband works well for a car often driven in the city, pulling strongly from stoplights and away from street corners; and in autocrossing, pulling hard out of tight course sections.

Four-into-one headers keep each cylinder's tube separate from the cylinder head to the end of the header, where all four tubes are welded to a larger collector which in turn is connected to the exhaust

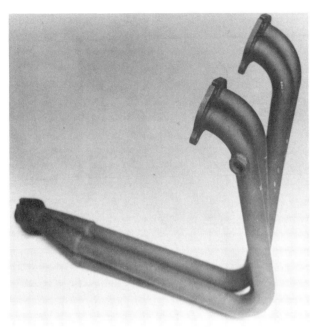

This Jackson Racing header for third-generation Civic and CRX is a typical four-into-one design. This arrangement is strongest in the high-rpm range. The 31 in. equal-length steel tubes are each 1½ in. in diameter. *Jackson Racing*

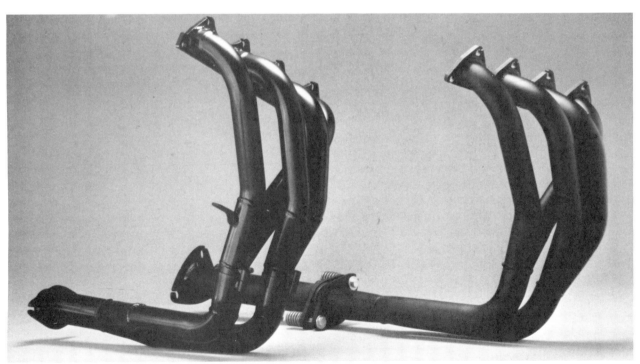

These Jackson Racing headers for the 1988 and 1989 Acura Integras, left, and 1988 and 1989 Honda CRX, right, are tri-Y designs. They augment the mid-rpm range. *Jackson Racing*

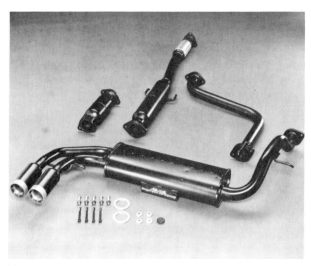

Mugen makes a sports silencer kit for the CRX 1988–90 that bolts into the existing stock mounts. The pipes are aluminized steel coated with a tough heat-resistant paint to battle corrosion. *King Motorsports*

system. This design can also be tuned for low-speed use, but is the configuration most common for racing and other high-speed use.

When choosing a header, speak to the supplier about it and make sure that it is compatible with your plans for the car and the other engine modifications you're making.

Turbo considerations

The exhaust requirements for turbocharged cars are somewhat different. Like naturally aspirated engines, turbo engines like a free exhaust system with minimal backpressure, but even more so. Backpressure creates resistance for the turbo's exhaust turbine, which in turn slows its spin-up time and holds back its top speed. The former increases lag, the interval between opening the throttle, and building boost and power; the latter limits power at high speeds.

Many turbo systems use the stock exhaust manifold or a specially cast manifold, rather than a header, for mounting or durability reasons. The rest of the exhaust system may need to handle greater flow than a high-performance system for a naturally aspirated engine, so look for a system designed for use with turbochargers, preferably for the specific turbo system you're using.

Valvetrain

While installing free-flowing intake and exhaust systems is important for increasing power, these improvements can be augmented by modifications to the valvetrain: the camshaft, rocker arms, valve springs and valves.

Installing a different cam is the most common of these changes and in most Hondas is straightforward. A high-performance camshaft generally has greater lift and duration than stock, and the timing may be different.

Cam lift

Lift has to do with the shape of the cam. An individual cam is oblong, serves a single valve and often is referred to as a cam lobe; the full string of lobes makes up the camshaft. A cam lobe works by having one end of a rocker arm follow it as it rotates. The rocker arm works like a teeter-totter; it has a pivot roughly in the middle (the rocker arm shaft), and rocks back and forth. The end of the rocker arm opposite the cam contacts the valve. So, as the taller portion of the lobe first reaches the rocker arm, the cam end of the arm pivots upward and the valve end of the rocker arm pivots downward, opening the valve.

When the tallest portion of the lobe is contacting the rocker arm, the valve is fully open. Tension between the valve, rocker arm and cam lobe is provided by the valve spring which is trying to close the valve. The distance the rocker arm moves upward at the cam lobe is the lift. Cam lift usually is increased by the rocker arm because the rocker arm shaft is skewed toward the cam side of the arm. This offset results in greater movement at the valve than at the cam.

Increasing intake valve lift makes a clearer path past the valve head and into the cylinder, encouraging more fuel and air to enter, while increasing exhaust valve lift clears the way for more thorough scavenging of the cylinder during the exhaust stroke. The result is higher power.

Cam duration

Duration is the length of time the valve stays open. It is measured in degrees of cam rotation; the cam rotates at half engine speed so 2 degrees of cam rotation equals 1 degree of crankshaft rotation. The longer the cam holds the intake valve open, the longer the time allowed for fuel and air to enter the cylinder. To complement the greater intake of fuel and air, the exhaust valve must stay open longer as well.

Comparing duration figures between camshafts is difficult because the exact points at which the measurements are taken vary from manufacturer to manufacturer. Generally, the measurement begins just after the valve opens and ends just before it closes, but there is no industry standard. In racing circles, 0.050 in. of lift is commonly used. But few cams intended for street use are measured this way. Their manufacturers start and end at lower lifts to

To fully exploit changes to the engine's intake and exhaust systems, the valvetrain can be improved. Shown are adjustable camshaft pulleys, various high-performance cam-shafts, bronze valve guides, high-rpm valve springs and stainless steel valves. *Jackson Racing*

Jackson Racing makes performance camshafts for the 1986–89 Integra. Designed for the twin-cam 1600 cc engine, these cams retain a smooth idle, good driveability and fine mileage, yet pump out a considerable power increase between 3000–7000 rpm. *Jackson Racing*

pump up the figures, making the cams seem to have more duration than those measured using conservative reference points.

Camshaft timing

Camshaft timing, also called valve timing, is also measured in degrees. Advancing or retarding the timing either through the grinding of a new camshaft or the use of an adjustable timing belt pulley on the cam can increase power somewhat, or shift the engine's strength to a higher or lower powerband. Using an adjustable pulley allows you to fine-tune your cam to your engine and its particular combination of components.

Other modifications

Other valvetrain modifications include adding larger valves and stronger valve springs. Larger valves free the flow of the intake fuel-air mixture and the exhaust gases, increasing power. Correspondingly larger valve seats are required; the operation requires substantial machine work and can be expensive.

Stronger valve springs are required for racing-type camshafts with much greater lift and duration than stock. These cams open and close the valves at much greater speed, requiring greater resistance from the springs. If the inertia of a quickly opening valve overcomes the resistance of the spring, the valve will open farther than intended, alter the valve timing and may bounce back off the valve seat when it closes. This is called valve float and can be damaging, particularly if the out-of-control valve careens into the upward-moving piston. Such a crash can destroy the engine.

Cylinder head

Several improvements can be made to the cylinder head although, like valve and valve seat enlargement, the machine work can be extensive and

Mugen makes a sport cam set-up for the 1986–89 Integras to increase horsepower throughout the rpm range of the engine. The camshafts are made from cast billets and retain the stock rocker arm geometry. The special valve springs are designed to work with the high-lift camshaft to curb any valve bounce. *King Motorsports*

expensive. For instance, the intake and exhaust ports can be enlarged and reshaped at strategic points. And the ports and combustion chambers can be polished. However, the exact size and shape of ports, and the surface finish of ports and combustion chambers, are open to wide discussion and experimentation.

One simple and inexpensive machining operation is available, however, and that is milling the cylinder head deck. By removing a small amount of material from the deck with a mill—say, 0.010 in.—the compression ratio will increase slightly. This is a common practice if for no other reason than to ensure that the deck is flat. The head should not be milled drastically, however, because the cam timing will be altered, and the head will be weakened and may warp.

Cylinder head milling is illegal in certain racing classes.

Flywheel

Lighter flywheels are sold for many Hondas. They will not increase power, but they can increase acceleration.

Consider the function of a flywheel and you'll understand the distinction. In an engine, power comes in jolts with each spark of the ignition. In a four-cylinder engine like those built by Honda, there are just two power strokes per revolution. Engineers smooth out these jolts by attaching a heavy wheel to the end of the crankshaft. The inertia from the wheel carries the crankshaft from one power pulse to the next, smoothing the passage of power.

For an example of how this works, quickly roll a tire along the ground for several yards. Then try to halt it. Chances are, the tire will roll on for several more feet before you can gain control; you have to overcome its inertia. This force must also be overcome if a wheel is to be speeded up. Using a tire as an example again, roll it along the ground as fast as you can in a single movement of your arms. Again, you need quite an effort to overcome the tire's inertia, or its tendency to stay in the state it's in (this time, standing still).

In the same way, the engine has to work hard to overcome the inertia of a heavy stock flywheel when it's accelerating. Substituting a lighter flywheel reduces the inertia the engine must overcome and results in quicker acceleration. It's like being asked to roll an air-filled tire instead of a concrete-filled tire. The lighter tire is far easier to put in motion. An engine with a light flywheel—either a stock one with excess weight machined off, or one made from lightweight aluminum rather than iron—may make the engine idle more roughly, make air conditioner operation more difficult at idle and make pulling away from an uphill stop a greater strain, but it will sharpen throttle response and quicken acceleration.

Compatibility

The temptation to order a catalog from every Honda specialist, and then pick and choose the trickest parts from each is tempting. And if this means choosing one specialist for suspension components, another for brakes and yet another for engine parts, the shopping around may pay off. However, if it means choosing valves from one company, valve springs from another and a camshaft from a third, trouble may be brewing. This approach is most likely to cause problems when choosing engine components (suspension components are a close second). Having parts that are compatible, that result in a good combination, can often be more important than having the latest development in pistons, valves, ignition, carburetion, exhaust and so on. If benefits from these parts are not complementary, the expected power increases will cancel out one another.

7

Putting power to the ground

Front-wheel-drive cars like Hondas are known for their traction advantage over front-engine, rear-wheel-drive cars. This ability to claw through snow and mud comes from concentrating the weight of the engine, and transmission and final-drive axle (transaxle) on the drive wheels at the front of the car. The greater the weight on these wheels, the greater the traction on slippery surfaces.

Unfortunately this advantage is reduced on high-grip surfaces like a smooth, dry asphalt road or racetrack. When accelerating hard on high-grip pavement, a great deal of the car's weight transfers from the front to the rear.

A properly fitted lightweight wheel such as this Revolution on Bob Endicott's CRX, coupled with a high-performance tire like this 205/60–13 Hoosier Autocrosser can make more difference in cornering power than any other modification to your Honda. The Hoosier Autocrosser, while carrying a US Department of Transportation stamp and thus being street legal, is too soft for daily street use. Hoosier does make a harder-compound version of the tire for the street, however.

The effect is illustrated by the nose of the car rising and the tail squatting. This rearward pitching lowers the weight on the front wheels just when they need every ounce pressing them to the pavement. The result, if the engine is powerful enough, will be wheel spin and lost acceleration. So, while front-drive is a traction champion under slippery, low-speed conditions, it's a tire-smoking underdog when the pavement's clean, dry and smooth.

Tires

The simplest way to increase the car's grip on the road—either under acceleration or while cornering—is to mount better tires. Family-oriented Hondas like the non-Si Civics and CRXs and the earlier Accords benefit the most because Honda specifies tires for them that are designed for low drag to ease the engine's job of overcoming the tire's rolling resistance and in turn raise fuel economy. Other principal requirements for these standard tires are long wear, low noise and smooth ride. For sport models like the CRX Si and Civic Si, the Prelude and Integra, and the third-generation Accord, Honda specifies tires whose attributes are skewed toward high grip, strong cornering performances and sure braking. But even these tires must be long-wearing and quiet, and perform well in wet as well as dry weather.

Great gains in traction can be found by those willing to trade tread longevity for softer, faster-wearing tires; rolling resistance for wider, stiffer tires that resist roll-under during hard cornering; and deep, multiple-ribbed tires for tires with fewer water-channeling grooves and larger, more-stable blocks of tread that won't twist away from the road when you tramp down on the throttle. It's also important to make sure that replacement tires have a sufficient speed rating. The rating assures you that the particular tire model has been tested to withstand a certain speed.

Another tire suitable for autocrossing or road racing that is also street-legal is the Yokohama A-008R. These 205/60-13 tires are mounted on 5 x 13 in. early Accord wheels and are used on the author's Civic 1200. The wheels were bought from a junkyard for $20 each. The tires are hard enough for limited daily driving but the partially slick tread works poorly in rain.

Although it's unlikely that you'll sustain the tire's rated speed on anything but a racetrack, speed ratings are another indicator of the tire's performance ability. The most commonly used portion of the rating scale is as follows:

S: up to 112 mph
T: up to 118 mph
H: up to 130 mph
V: up to 149 mph
Z: more than 149 mph

For high performance, tires with an H rating or higher are generally used. The rating is included in the tire's size. For instance, a 175/70HR-13 tire has an H speed rating; the R stands for radial construction, by far the most common type for high-performance tires.

In the 1970s, choosing a high-performance tire was fairly easy. Then, you looked for one of the top two or three European brands and chose that company's performance tire. As automotive performance began its resurgence in the early 1980s, and autocrossing and Showroom Stock racing became a place for tire companies to show their engineering expertise on street-legal tires, the choice became harder and harder. Not only have more companies with more tire models entered the high-performance market, now they improve the tires or bring out new models yearly.

With such competition, the hot tire can change month by month. The good news is that plenty of high-performance tires are available. The bad news is that it's hard to zero in on the best. Read automotive magazines, particularly those that cover autocrossing and road racing, to keep track of the tire trends. Read the articles and advertisements, and see which tires are winning.

It may not give you the answer, however, because, like Honda, you may wish to make some compromises of your own if all-out performance is not your only goal. As with the rest of the car, set your expectations and then plan the means to meet them. For instance, consider how important tread wear is. A standard tire should be good for 40,000 miles. The softer rubber of a high-performance tire may wear out in 20,000. Is that acceptable? Or maybe you can afford to replace the tires every 10,000 miles or so. If so, then the extra-soft, racing version is what you want.

Most manufacturers indicate their street-legal racing tires by an additional letter in the model name. For instance, General designates its racing tires with the letter G, as in the XP 2000 G. Goodyear uses the letter S for its Eagle ZRS and Eagle VRS tires. Most other companies have chosen the letter R. Examples include the B. F. Goodrich Comp T/A R1, Toyo 4DR, and Yokohama A001-R, A008-R and A008-RTU. Bridgestone straddles the alphabetical track with its RE61S and RE71R.

Where you live and drive plays an important role in tires used on the street. If you're a desert dweller, a lightly treaded tire like the partially slick Yokohama 008 or 008-R might be just the thing. But if rain is a regular way of life in your area, a fully treaded tire is required. Those in the North who make a practice of installing another set of tires when the weather turns cold may be able to get away with skimpy racing treads in the summer and aggressively treaded snow tires in the winter. High-performance snow and ice tires are sold as well, as are studs for ice racing and rallying. Most come from Europe where winter racing on street-type tires is a way of life. Look to magazines that cover rallying and ice racing for tips for the latest, most effective winter tires. If you do change to winter tires, mount them on all four wheels.

Tire sizing

Diameter and width are important considerations when choosing new tires, and performance can be improved by varying from the standard sizes. But make sure you understand tire sizing before making a choice. A typical Honda tire size is 175/70-13. The figure 175 means that, inflated, the tire is 175 mm wide from sidewall to sidewall. This is called the section width; if you cut a section out of the tire, and compensate for the expanding effect of inflation, this is how wide the section of tire will be.

The figure 13 means that the tire must be mounted on a 13 in. diameter wheel.

The figure 70 indicates that the section height—the distance from the edge of the wheel to the top of the tread—is seventy percent of the tire's section width. This is called the aspect ratio, and a tire with a seventy percent aspect ratio is commonly called a 70 series tire; one with a sixty percent aspect ratio is called a 60 series tire and so on.

With these figures, you can calculate the tire's diameter. To do so, multiply the section width of 175 mm by the aspect ratio of 0.70. The product is 122.5 mm, the section height. Converted to inches (122.5 mm times 0.039 in. per mm), the section height is 4.78 in. So, to get the overall height of the tire, add the 4.78 in. height from the road to the rim, the 13 in. diameter of the wheel and the additional 4.78 in. of height from the top of the wheel to the top of the tire. The overall diameter (its height) adds up to 22.56 in. Although the exact width and diameter might vary by a quarter inch or so from brand to brand because of design differences, the tire's diameter is a worthwhile reference for comparing tires of different aspect ratio and wheel diameter.

Keeping the tire diameter about the same as stock is important for several reasons. First, an excessively tall tire may rub the top of the fender wells. Second, a tire whose diameter varies from stock will make the speedometer and odometer inaccurate. A shorter tire will make the meters read too high; a taller tire will make them read too low. And third, an excessively short tire will look odd but more importantly will have a reduced contact patch—the area of the tire contacting the road, reducing traction over a taller tire of the same type.

The width of a tire is important because the contact patch is greater with a wider tire as well, increasing potential traction. The aspect ratio is important because a lower aspect ratio generally will result in a tire more resistant to sidewall roll-under. If the tire's sidewall is not stiff enough to stay upright during cornering, it will roll under and the tire will be rolling on the sidewall rather than the tread, reducing contact patch and traction. The design of the tire has much to do with a tire's ability to resist roll-under, but among high-performance tires the aspect ratio is a reasonable gauge.

Switching to wider tires

To apply this to a real Honda, say you have an early Civic that came with 155SR–12 tires (when the aspect ratio is missing from the size, consider it to be eighty percent or 80 series). You want to retain the stock wheels and tire diameter, but increase the tire width somewhat and reduce the aspect ratio to seventy percent to increase traction. First, figure the original tire's section height; since the wheel diameter will remain the same, the section height must remain the same as well to achieve the original tire diameter. To figure the section height, multiply the section width of 155 mm times the aspect ratio of 0.80 times the metric conversion factor of 0.039 in. per mm. The section height multiplies out to 4.84 in.

With the diameter in hand, work backward to figure the width of a 70 series tire with about the same section height. Divide the section height of 4.84 in. by the desired aspect ratio of 0.70, and divide the result by the metric conversion factor of 0.039 in. per mm. From this, the optimum tire width is 177.3 mm. And as luck would have it, a few tire makers produce 175/70–12 tires.

For those who resist wrestling with a calculator to come up with sizes this way, here's a good rule of thumb: For every ten percentage points you reduce the aspect ratio, add 20 mm in section width. Using a 165–13 tire (with an aspect ratio of 80) as an example, a 185/70–13 will yield approximately the same tire diameter; so will a 205/60–13.

Wheels

A quick comparison of different Hondas shows that as the performance level rises, say from a standard model to an Si model, Honda follows the pattern just discussed with one exception. While Honda also uses a wider section width, lower aspect ratio and same tire diameter, it also increases the wheel diameter. Compare, for instance, the standard 1989 CRX to the 1989 CRX Si. The standard CRX calls

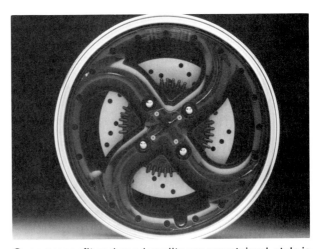

Once proper fit and good quality are ascertained, style is the only remaining point to be decided. This Dragon wheel, sold by Jackson racing, is a three-piece design that weighs just 12 pounds. It fits several late-model Hondas. *Jackson Racing*

The Mugen MR-5 wheels are two-piece units available in three sizes to match most Hondas. The rims are cast aluminum bolted to forged aluminum centers. *King Motorsports*

for 175/70-13 tires; these tires have a diameter of 22.68 in. The CRX Si calls for 185/60-14 tires; their diameter is essentially the same at 22.66 in.

You can make a good argument that if Honda wanted to use 60 series tires on the Si, it should have just added 20 mm to the section width and mounted 195/60-13s. But, besides being a hard-to-find size, there's a problem with that approach if carried too far. As the section width gets wider, the clearance between the tire sidewall, and the wheelwell and the suspension components disappears quickly. This is particularly true with the strut-type and strut-derived suspensions used by so many Hondas.

Plus system

The idea is to lower the aspect ratio for better cornering and add a moderate amount of section width. Then, to keep the tire diameter the same as original, increase the wheel diameter. This process is commonly known as the Plus One or Plus Two concept, meaning that if you reduce the aspect ratio ten percent you must add one inch to the wheel diameter (Plus One) and 10 mm to the section width; if you reduce the aspect ratio twenty percent, add two inches to the wheel diameter (Plus Two) and 20 mm to the section width.

The rule of thumb in this case is to add 10 mm of section width and one inch of wheel diameter for each ten percent reduction in aspect ratio. So a 175/70-13, a 185/60-14 and a 195/50-15 all have approximately the same tire diameter yet different wheel diameters.

Wheel sizing

Offset is an important dimension to consider when replacing wheels. Offset is the amount of wheel width to the inside of the brake hub's wheel-mounting surface minus the amount to the outside of the surface. Improper offset can make the steering react unpredictably to changes in surface (for example, when one front tire is on dry pavement and the other enters a puddle of water). It also can make the suspension track poorly over bumps; cause interference between the wheels, and the wheelwells or suspension, or wear out wheel bearings prematurely. Make sure replacement wheels have the same offset as the wheels that came on the car. Wheels with proper offset were hard to find before front-wheel-drive cars became popular, but the success of Honda and others with front-wheel drive has pretty well solved that problem.

In fact, there's a nearly endless selection of special wheels that fit all but the earliest Hondas properly. Most are made from aluminum alloy; these are commonly called alloy wheels. All Hondas have four lugs per wheel. And all Hondas use studs on the wheel hubs and nuts to retain the wheels. But early Hondas—all first-generation Civics and first-generation Accords—have a wide, 120 mm bolt circle. The bolt circle is calculated by measuring from the center of the brake hub to the center of any of the studs; the radius of a circle drawn through the centers of the studs will have the same dimension. The bolt circle is also known as the bolt pattern when the number of lugs is included (for example, 4x120 mm).

While the selection of wheels with the 4x120 mm pattern is limited, there are several options. The least expensive is to scour junkyards for a set of 1981 Accord four-door wheels. They are steel and measure 13 in. in diameter by 5 in. in width. Tires in 175/70-13, 185/70-13 and 185/60-13 sizes will work fine on this wheel. BWA (13x5) and Panasport (13x6) offer aluminum alloy wheels in the early pattern and proper size and offset, and will drill them to the 120 mm bolt pattern at the factory on special order. So, if a particular design catches your fancy, inquire with the dealer or directly to the factory to see if this service is offered.

Second-generation Civics and Accords, and all subsequent Hondas use a narrower and much more common 100 mm bolt circle. Wheels are plentiful for this pattern; the selection is in fact overwhelming. As with the early Hondas, a good inexpensive solution is to shop the junkyards. The aluminum wheels from a CRX Si or Civic Si make a good upgrade for Civics and CRXs equipped with factory steel wheels. The sizes are 13x5 and 14x5, and are cast into the wheels. Search for aluminum Prelude or Accord wheels to replace the steel equivalents as well. For individuality of design or greater width, though, look to other wheel manufacturers. When doing so, the main considerations besides offset are width and weight.

By choosing a relatively wide wheel for the tire being used, the sidewall is stretched tautly, inhibiting roll-under. Once you've decided on a tire size, make and model, check the wheel widths recommended for it by the manufacturer; the dealer should have a list. Look for wheels on the wide end of the range. For an idea of the ranges you can encounter, a typical 175/70-13 tire is rated for wheels between 5 and 6 in. wide. A 185/60-14 typically calls for a wheel between 5 and 6.5 in. wide. A 195/50-15 normally requires a wheel between 5.5 and 7 in. wide.

Reducing wheel weight can significantly improve the suspension's ability to follow bumps and dips in the road. All components between the springs and the road, including the wheels, tires and most of the suspension, are unsprung. Their weight is called unsprung weight. The lower the unsprung weight, the less inertia there is to overcome, making the suspension's job—particularly the shock absorbers—easier. The simple, lightweight suspension components of most Hondas contribute to the cars' high handling capabilities.

The easiest way to reduce unsprung weight further is to install lighter wheels. When doing so, make sure that the wheels are intended for street use if that is how your car is used. Some wheels are so light that they can be used only for racing; the potholes of everyday streets will bend or break their thin, aluminum alloy walls.

There's another benefit to using lightweight wheels: reduction of rotational inertia. Using light road wheels is like using a lightened flywheel on the engine but, in a way, four times more effective since you're lightening four wheels.

Beyond these considerations, let style be your final guide in selecting a new wheel.

Brakes

Looking for ways to improve brakes can lead Honda owners into a quandary. Even though most Hondas use disk brakes in front and drum brakes in the rear, only a few modifications are needed for high-performance or even competition use.

Installing high-performance front pads is by far the most cost-effective change that can be made to a Honda braking system. Several brands are sold; Repco Metalmasters are probably the most popular, and strike a good balance between increased brake-fade resistance and quick warm-up. Harder pads like those used for road racing are desirable in competition for their high heat resistance but must reach a certain temperature to work properly. This warming-up requirement makes them unusable on the street or in time trials like autocrosses.

Brake upgrades can include these Repco high-temperature pads and drilled and vented rotors, among other modifications. The workmanship here is beautiful. *Jackson Racing*

Drilled or grooved disk brake rotors are sold for Hondas, and can improve braking by increasing the flow of air through the disk for better cooling. The holes or grooves also release trapped brake dust, improving performance. These parts are suitable for street use, but often will move a car into a higher category when used in competition.

Disk brakes can be added to the rear of some Hondas by buying new parts for later models or buying used parts at junkyards. But for street purposes the gain is insignificant and for competition the conversion is generally illegal (in the classes the conversion is allowed, racing brakes make more sense).

In the same way, ventilated front brake rotors can be added to some Hondas that came with solid rotors. An example is the first-generation Civic that came with solid rotors; the station wagon came with ventilated rotors. By swapping the full front braking system from a Civic station wagon to a hatchback or sedan, some improvement can be seen. This also applies to the second-generation Civics in which the 1983 1500s had ventilated rotors. This is a worthwhile swap for a street car, although a fair amount of work and expense is involved. If the car is used for competition, make sure the swap is legal in the intended class.

Replacing the stock flexible brake hoses with steel braided hoses can improve brake pedal feel, reducing pedal play for more exact brake control. They also are more durable. Extremely high temperature brake fluid can improve brake performance by eliminating fluid boiling. Ducting air to the front brakes can greatly increase their resistance to fade by cooling the brakes better. No kits are sold for this, although ducts and high-temperature flexible tubing are sold by racing suppliers to connect custom-made brake shrouding to customized air dams. This sort of ducting is standard procedure for Improved Touring racing, and makes sense for street use since few mechanical changes are made, and day-to-day operation is unaltered.

Transaxle

The sort of advantage that using brakes from a slightly different model within the same model generation can bring to Honda brake systems can also be realized by mixing and matching transaxles. This is most helpful for Hondas geared for high fuel economy: by choosing a transaxle with a lower final-drive gear ratio (higher numerically), acceleration will be improved. Also, look for a relatively close-ratio gear set, one in which the ratio change from gear to gear is relatively small. Because engine power rises with rpm until the power peak is reached, close-ratio gears can improve acceleration by reducing the drop in rpm between upshifts; with each shift, the engine is closer to the power peak.

For example, a 1978 or 1979 Civic CVCC could take advantage of an earlier transaxle which has somewhat closer gear spacing and a much lower final-drive ratio. The 1978–1979 transaxle has first through fifth gear ratios of 3.181:1, 1.823:1, 1.181:1, 0.846:1 and 0.714:1, and a final-drive ratio in most applications of 3.875:1. In comparison, the 1975 transaxle has first through fifth gear ratios of 3.000:1, 1.789:1, 1.182:1, 0.846:1 and 0.655:1, and a final-drive ratio of 4.733:1. Only the fifth gear of the 1975 transaxle is higher than that of the 1978–1979 transaxle, and the low final-drive ratio more than compensates for that.

The third-generation Civics and CRXs, in the non-Si versions, can gain acceleration simply by swapping to an Si transaxle, which has a lower final-drive ratio. Take the 1985 models, for example. The standard Civic 1500 has a final-drive ratio of 4.066:1, and the carbureted CRX and the Civic S have a ratio of 4.266:1, while the final-drive ratio for the CRX Si is 4.428:1. This lower ratio will make a noticeable difference in a carbureted CRX or Civic S, and a substantial change in the standard Civic.

It is possible to buy the final-drive gears for the CRX Si, and install them in one of the other transaxles, but from the standpoint of labor and cost, it's often more practical to find a used transaxle with the desired gears and install it as unit. In fact, both the Si engine and transaxle make a good swap for a standard trim CRX or Civic because these bodies carry fewer weight-adding options.

Transaxle swaps such as these can be beneficial, depending on how your car is geared, and whether you can find a more desirably geared version in a junkyard in good condition and for a reasonable price. Consult the specification charts for the ratios.

When considering a swap, always stay within the same model range and generation to ensure compatibility; mounts and bolt patterns vary from model to model and generation to generation.

Used transaxles are also a good way to upgrade from a four-speed to a five-speed. This change does not result in quicker acceleration in most cases because Honda four-speed transaxles generally are geared like the five-speeds minus the fifth gear. Fifth gear almost always is an extra-high overdrive. But with a transaxle that uses low final-drive gearing, the fifth gear can make highway driving much more relaxed because the engine runs at lower rpm.

Special close-ratio gear sets can be bought for some Honda transaxles but are expensive, even without the cost of dismantling the transaxle to install them. For some cars, particularly those used in high-level competition or for an ultimate street Honda, they make sense because of their extremely low rpm drop between shifts.

Limited-slip differential

If you are willing to delve inside your transaxle, or pay someone else to do so, you may want to consider a limited-slip differential. The differential is the component that allows the driven wheels to rotate at different speeds when the car is turning. A standard differential will drive one of the front

A limited-slip differential can reduce wheelspin, which is hard to control in high-powered front-wheel-drive cars like modified Hondas. This diff is built for competition-only use in Civics and CRXs. *Jackson Racing*

wheels while the other freewheels; this freewheeling is also called slippage. A limited-slip differential uses clutches to connect the front wheels and limit the freewheeling to the minimum required for smooth turning. The clutches connect the wheels firmly enough so that tire spin will not occur until the traction of both front tires is overcome.

With a standard differential, acceleration is limited by the traction available from a single tire. This poses a particular problem when accelerating hard out of a corner: the inside front wheel has relatively little weight on it because the car's weight is transferred to the outside, so that wheel is easy to spin. A limited-slip differential can make quite a difference in competition, particularly in autocrossing which has tight turns that are often exited in first or second gear. Think twice about using a limited-slip differential on the street, however, as torque steer and steering-wheel fight may increase. And the units are expensive.

Clutch

Consider this. First, for quick acceleration, you build a strong engine for your Honda—multiple carburetors, raised compression and more aggressive valve timing, or maybe a turbo system. Second, you select the widest, stickiest tires that will fit the car properly. Third, you install a transaxle with low gearing and a limited-slip differential to make full use of the engine's power and the tires' grip. You'd think your rocketship Honda is ready to launch. But there's one weak link in the power-to-the-pavement chain that needs to be beefed up: the clutch, the component that links the engine to the transaxle.

Under this scenario, a stronger high-performance clutch is vital. Most Honda specialists sell such clutches. There are two common types. The first, usually described as a heavy-duty clutch, looks much like a stock Honda clutch. One difference is a stronger pressure plate. This component's spidery, diaphragm-type spring clamps the clutch disk to the flywheel with greater force to reliably transmit increased power from the engine's crankshaft into the transaxle's input shaft. Another difference is the clutch disk whose friction surface is stronger and has a superior resistance to heat. The greater clamping

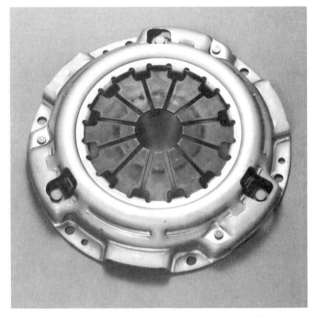

The Mugen sports clutch is made for 1988–90 CRXs and Civics. While this unit is designed for high-performance use and autocrossing, it is streetable and does not cause high pedal pressure. *King Motorsports*

A heavy-duty clutch such as this is needed when power and traction are increased. *Jackson Racing*

The Centerforce clutch increases clamping power by using weights mounted on a ring around the center of the pressure plate to increase pressure on the clutch disc as the rpm rise. This method keeps clutch pedal pressure down. *Jackson Racing*

119

force of the pressure plate combined with the clutch disk's improvements result in sure coupling of the engine and transaxle.

The second type of clutch carries the brand name Centerforce and also looks much like a stock Honda clutch, with one exception: a wire ring encircles the diaphragm near its outer edge. Attached to the ring between each finger of the diaphragm are weights. As the rpm rises, centrifugal force acts on the weights, increasing the pressure plate's clamping force. This system produces strong clamping without an overly heavy spring and the high clutch pedal pressure needed to disengage a strongly sprung clutch.

For stock or nearly stock engines, Honda's clutches are fine and provide long life. And because of competition rules, they are required for certain classes. When using a stock clutch in competition, it's wise to remove and inspect the clutch more often than normal as part of a maintenance routine for inspecting all the car's mechanical components. The frequency of inspection depends on the car's use. For endurance road racing, it should be checked every race. For sprint road racing or a heavy schedule of autocrossing, yearly inspection may make sense. For street use and occasional autocrossing, keep the clutch properly adjusted and inspect it if frequent or large adjustments become necessary.

8

Handling and suspension

You can have the strongest engine, the best brakes and the most ideal wheel-and-tire combination, and still not have a high-performance Honda. The ability to accelerate and stop quickly is wasted without the final member of the high-performance triad: handling. The car must cut through corners cleanly because nearly all roads turn left or right at some point, and good handling balance can do more to bring out the pleasure of sports driving than any other factor.

Tires

High-performance tires can improve handling more than any other single change and, for that matter, more than several changes in some cases. The reason is simple: The tires connect the car to the ground. The stronger the connection, the better handling. So great strides can be made by adding high-performance tires, and even greater improvements can be achieved by using competition versions of these tires with soft rubber compounds (make

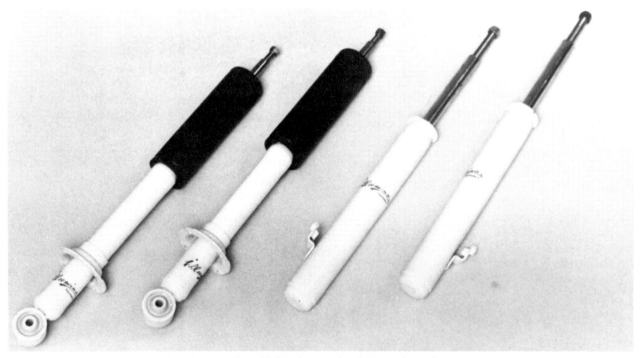

Adjustable struts and shock absorbers such as Tokico's Illuminas allow the handling of the car to be tailored from track to track, or from street to track, with the twist of a screwdriver. *Jackson Racing*

sure the tire has a DOT stamp, showing that it meets US Department of Transportation standards for street use). But, remember, as explained earlier, these tires can result in deterioration of wet-weather performance, tread wear and ride, and may produce more road noise.

Shock absorbers

The shock absorbers, integral parts of the suspension struts in most Hondas, resist the up-and-down movement of the wheels and attached suspension parts. That may seem odd in light of the argument to reduce unsprung weight to allow the suspension to move more freely, and speed its reaction to bumps and dips in the road. And in some respects reducing unsprung weight, say, by using lighter wheels, allows shock absorbers of lower resistance to be used. But, overall, reducing unsprung weight and increasing shock absorber resistance are parts of the same battle to fight the inertia of unsprung components. Additionally, the shock absorbers work to control the movement of the car

body as it traverses bumps and dips, pitches backward and forward under acceleration and braking, and rolls to the outside under cornering.

As with tires, Honda designs its shock absorbers to a compromised set of specifications; performance must be balanced against a smooth ride. Shocks that deliver the utmost in performance provide great resistance; they are stiff.

One extreme is using no shocks at all, which results in a car that bounds in response to the smallest of rises and dips. This provides a smooth ride but the roller-coaster motion results in a trajectory no more accurate than a pogo stick's.

Another extreme is shocks tuned to racing stiffness. Designed for racetracks with no potholes or bumps, just smooth curves and gradual rises and falls, these shocks create so much resistance to suspension movement that running over a small rock feels like crashing over a curb in a normal car.

The goal is to find shock absorbers tuned somewhere between these extremes. For high-performance use, of course, the compromise should be

Anti-roll bars assist the springs in controlling body roll. While stock anti-roll bars are generally small in diameter and suspended in rubber bushings, this bar on Angelo Roberson's Civic 1200 is beefy and mounted in metal blocks. It also substitutes for the stock front radius rods,

which have been removed. This arrangement, in which the struts are located side to side by a lower suspension link, and front to back by the anti-roll bar, is the original Mac-Pherson Strut set-up. It's simple, light and effective.

closer to the racing settings but still provide enough compliance for practical street driving.

There are two general types of high-performance shock absorbers available: non-adjustable and adjustable. The non-adjustable high-performance shocks are similar to the stock units but stiffer. Some claim more sophisticated design or greater longevity. But their foremost purpose is to add more resistance to the suspension and give the car a sort of tied-down feeling that sharpens its reflexes, making it respond more surely when the steering wheel is turned.

The main parts of a shock absorber are its main tube, filled with hydraulic fluid, a rod that connects to the body on one end and a piston that rides within the tube on the other end; one end of the tube connects to the suspension. The piston contains small holes that are sized to allow a particular amount of fluid to pass through the piston and valves that open when hydraulic pressure from movement of the piston in the fluid reaches a certain speed. By reducing the orifice sizes or increasing the pressure at which the valves open, the stiffness of the shock absorber can be increased. By changing just one or the other, the shock can be tuned for specific high-performance results. This tuning is commonly called valving a shock absorber.

Adjustable shocks are just like non-adjustable except that their valving can be changed by turning a knob on the end of the shock. Some adjustable shocks must be partially removed to make the changes which, depending on the work involved, defeats the adjustable shock's greatest advantage: the ability to change from near-race-level stiffness to a near-boulevard ride at a moment's notice. In practice, you might adjust the shocks stiff for a drive through the mountains or for an autocross, and then loosen them up when returning to city or highway driving.

Gas-pressurized shocks

Many shock absorbers, both standard and high-performance, are now gas-pressurized. By pumping nitrogen into the shock absorber under pressure, aeration can be reduced. This foaming of the hydraulic fluid often led to shock absorber fade in older-design shocks in racing cars. Foaming reduces a shock absorber's effectiveness because air bubbles can be compressed, while the shock relies on the fact that its hydraulic fluid cannot be compressed. (A column of fluid in a tube topped off with a well-sealed piston, with no valves or orifices, is solid; the piston cannot make the column of fluid shorter.) All of the engineers' careful calibrations are distorted and become meaningless when air infiltrates the fluid. However, improvements in the fluid and gas pressurization have reduced this problem greatly.

Anti-roll bars

Anti-roll bars are common on Hondas, but mostly at the front. Generally, just the Si models have rear anti-roll bars. The purpose of an anti-roll bar is to resist the car body's roll toward the outside of a corner. This also is one of the purposes of the car's springs, but relying on the springs alone for roll resistance results in a car that is sprung so stiffly that it reacts harshly to bumps. The advantage of using anti-roll bars is that they come into play only when

Mugen makes road racing stabilizer bars for 1984–87 Civics and CRXs and Integras. For road racing, the bars are available in both 23 and 25 mm sizes. Streetable stabilizer bars are also available from Mugen in 20, 21 and 22 mm sizes. *King Motorsports*

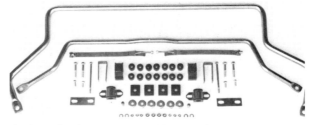

Jackson Racing makes stabilizer kits for both the Integra and CRX. The spring steel bars are oil-hardened and heat-tempered, providing maximum torsional strength. Stabilizer bars do not effect straight-line ride in cars; instead, they reduce body roll and improve steering response and control. The kits include polyurethane bushings and all necessary hardware. *Jackson Racing*

the car is turning, allowing the use of relatively soft springs for improved ride.

An anti-roll bar is a torsion bar, a kind of spring that resists being twisted, and returns to its original shape and orientation after being twisted. Anti-roll bars generally are U-shaped. The bottom of the U runs across the car and is attached to a subframe or

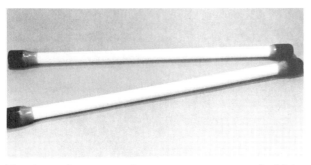

Heavier springs are an important component of a high-performance suspension system. In the case of the third-generation Civic and CRX, large-diameter torsion bars like these from Jackson Racing are required for the front suspension. *Jackson Racing*

To compensate for the lowering of his Civic, Angelo Roberson fabricated these spacers for the steering arms and tie rods.

the body by a pair of rubber bushings. The arms of the U run either forward or rearward, depending on how the bar is mounted, and are attached to the suspension by a link or bushing. The attachment of the rear anti-roll bar on the 1984–87 Civics and CRXs, and the first-generation Integra is different; it is located in the rear axle tube, but it also is a torsion bar with the same effect as a conventionally mounted anti-roll bar.

Here's an example of how an anti-roll bar works. In this case, assume it's a front anti-roll bar on a car making a left-hand turn. As the car begins to turn, the body starts rolling. If you were to look at the car, the right wheel would be tucked up into its wheelwell while the left wheel would be extending downward, away from its wheelwell; the body would be rolled to the right. In response, the right-side suspension will have moved upward. The left-side suspension will have moved downward. These opposite directions of movement will twist the anti-roll bar. Since the bar is a spring, it will resist the twisting, in turn using its resistance to help limit the roll. The more the car body tries to roll on its suspension, the more resistance the anti-roll bar will contribute. Adding a larger-diameter (stiffer) bar will increase the body's roll resistance.

In some ways there is little choice among different anti-roll bars. They all work on the same principle. However, the quality does vary from manufacturer to manufacturer. If you can, inspect the bar and its mounting hardware. They should be substantial, complete and include instructions. Also, if possible, speak with others who have changed anti-roll bars on their Hondas; reputation is a good guide in making a choice.

One other factor is adjustability. A few adjustable anti-roll bars are made for Hondas. By allowing the bar's connecting links to be installed in various locations along the legs of the U, the leverage on the bar can be adjusted, changing its stiffness.

Springs

As noted previously, simply using stiffer springs will increase a car's resistance to body roll, but to achieve roll resistance appropriate for a high-performance car without stiff anti-roll bars would require overly stiff springs.

High-performance springs are valuable, however. First, increasing the spring stiffness modestly will reduce body dive under braking or rear-end squat under acceleration. It will also increase roll resistance somewhat and result in a car with sharper reflexes that is easier to control under acceleration, turning and braking. Springs sold by Honda tuners are often shorter than stock, lowering the car an inch or so. This results in a lower center of gravity, improving handling as well.

Lowering

Hondas generally should not be lowered more than 1.5 in. because most Hondas have relatively short suspension travel. If the car is lowered too much, it will run out of suspension travel, crashing into the suspension stops over bumps or when cornering, greatly affecting the car's ride and handling. Additionally, if the car is lowered too far, the suspension links and control arms will operate at angles beyond their intended range, upsetting the relationship between the steering and suspension components in some cases, or disturbing the suspension geometry. When this relationship of the suspension components to one another is altered greatly, the handling can deteriorate rather than improve.

While special struts with lowered springs seats are sold for a few Hondas, the most common way to lower a Honda is with shorter, stiffer springs. If you buy short springs from a Honda specialist, installation should be straightforward. Each of the original springs must be compressed in turn, its strut must be removed and the spring must be removed from the strut. Then the replacement spring must be compressed and installed on the strut, and the strut must be reinstalled. This procedure must be repeated for the other three springs. If you are considering new springs and struts, replace them at the same time to avoid removing and replacing the struts twice.

Lowering the front of a 1984–87 Civic or CRX is easier because the front suspension is sprung with torsion bars that are height-adjustable. The height can be lowered by turning the height-adjustment nuts connected to the torsion bars. Larger-diameter torsion bars must be installed to increase the stiffness of the front springs, however. And because the rear of these cars is sprung with coil springs, the conventional route of using shorter springs must be followed to lower the rear end.

Springs can be custom-made for those who wish to experiment with springs beyond the range available from Honda tuners. Spring shops can wind coil springs with various wire thicknesses, number of coil and length. These shops usually can be found in large cities, and often work primarily with trucks and trailers.

Take great care whenever you remove or install suspension springs, particularly the strut-mounted type used on many Hondas. Even when the suspension is fully extended, the springs exert high pressure against their seats; they are still compressed. If you remove or install springs, make sure you read and thoroughly understand the procedure in the service manual for your car. Use a spring compressor and make sure you understand its operation beforehand. A mishandled spring that breaks loose from the suspension or a spring compressor can be deadly.

Suspension bushings

Stiffer bushings are available to replace the synthetic rubber bushings in certain suspension components, most often the mounting brackets for anti-roll bars. These high-performance bushings deflect less under heavy suspension loads because they're made of polyurethane (a pliable plastic that is stiffer than synthetic rubber but retains some of its noise

During road racing or autocrossing, the stock rubber suspension bushings will deflect and hurt response. Mugen developed hard rubber bushing kits to fit 1989–90 Civics and CRXs. *King Motorsports*

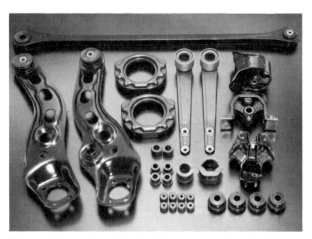

Mugen also makes a hard rubber suspension bushing kit for the earlier 1984–87 CRX and Civic. *King Motorsports*

insulation abilities), hard plastic (Delrin is a common example) or metal.

As with so many other high-performance suspension components, stiffer or solid bushings transmit harshness and additional sound into the car, making day-to-day driving less comfortable. But they also have the advantages of providing greater precision and quicker steering response.

Camber-caster plates

While many Hondas used MacPherson struts, only one of the three alignment settings—toe—can be adjusted. For high-performance use, the ability to adjust camber and caster is desirable as well, particularly on the front suspension. Camber-caster plates provide these adjustments, and usually replace the upper mounting and bushing at the top of the fender well where the strut rod is connected to the body.

Camber is the amount the top of the tire leans inward or outward in comparison to the bottom of the tire with the tires straight ahead. If the wheel leans inward at the top, it has negative camber. If it leans outward at the top, it has positive camber. The measurement is made in degrees and minutes.

Most Hondas will work better under hard cornering with negative camber. By leaning the wheel inward at the top, the bottom is leaned outward. This outward tilt where the tread meets the pavement helps resist tire-sidewall rollover, keeping more of the tread in contact with the road and increasing its cornering traction. Looked at another way, it gives the tire a head start against body and tire roll.

The disadvantage of negative camber, particularly in great amounts, say, more than one degree, is that tire wear will increase (on the inside edge) as the car is driven under normal conditions. Also, the car may dart when it encounters different surfaces from side to side, like running through a puddle with one side of the car.

Caster is hard to visualize on a car because of the links, arms and struts that make up the suspension. But, using a motorcycle as an example, think of the front forks and how the bottoms of the forks are ahead of the tops. The more the forks are leaned forward at the bottom, the greater the caster. The result when the handlebars are turned is that the bottom of the tire leans outward.

The alignment of car suspension components results in the same effect. The more the wheel on the outside of a corner is turned, the more the bottom of the tire leans outward. By adding more caster this effect is increased, again helping the tire tread to keep full contact against the road. Additionally, more caster increases the car's resistance to wandering when being driven straight, and increases the self-centering action of the steering wheel. The disadvan-

Camber-castor plates allow adjustment of front suspension alignment beyond that allowed by the stock components. Generally, toe is the only adjustment that can be made. This from A-T Engineering plate is installed on a Civic 1200.

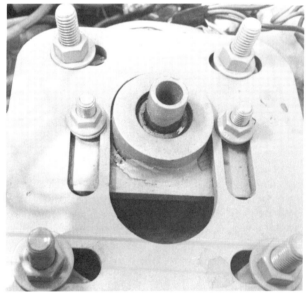

This plate differs mainly in attachment and is installed on George Cleveland's 1200 Civic. In addition to adding adjustments to the cars, these plates also attach to the strut rods with spherical bearings. These bearings replace the less precise synthetic rubber bushings that are stock.

tage of adding caster is that the wheel is harder to turn at slow speeds, particularly when parking.

Suspension kits

Most suspension kits consist of new shock absorbers or struts, anti-roll bars and springs. They have two advantages. First, the components are often less expensive in a kit than when purchased separately. Second, the components are matched to one another and are more likely to provide a good han-dling balance than components that are mixed and matched from different suppliers.

If you intend to completely redo your suspension for top performance, buying a full kit is the best way to modify the suspension. A possible exception is racers who have the time and facilities to test individual components. Even then, if the racer does not have sufficient equipment to measure the results of the changes, fails to conduct the testing consist-

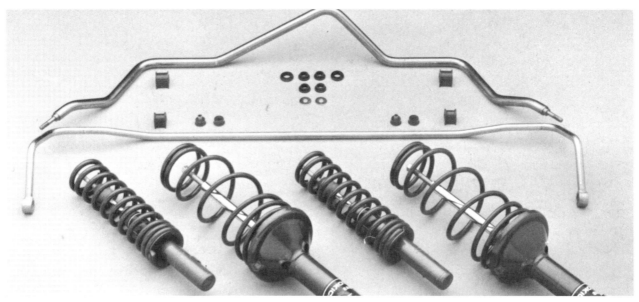

Buying a full suspension kit often makes the most sense, as each component should be compatible with one another. Also, when buying a full kit, the cost is often lower than buying the components separately. *Jackson Racing*

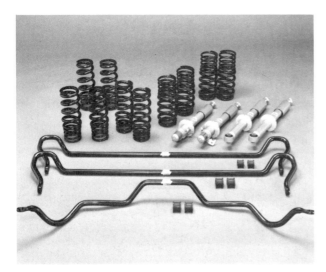

The Mugen sports suspension kit includes front and rear anti-roll bars, stiffer springs and shocks. The kit is avail-able for 1988–90 CRXs and Integras. *King Motorsports*

The Mugen sports damper kit is built in cooperation with Showa and is available for the 1988–89 CRX and Civic. The kit provides taut driving on the street. *King Motorsports*

When adjusting tire pressures to fine tune handling, a good indicator of pressure is a stripe of white shoe polish across the juncture of the tread and sidewall. After a run on a race or test course, the stripe should be worn off the tread but not the sidewall. If part of the stripe remains on the tread, reduce pressure. If part of the stripe is worn off the sidewall, increase pressure.

ently or does not log the information in a scientific manner, a suspension kit may prove superior.

Suspension tuning

It's possible to tune the suspension yourself and gain substantial handling improvements. But as already explained, a few testing mistakes can bring on a mediocre result or, for street cars, a dangerous handling balance. Your attitude toward driving safety, and understanding that what's best for an autocross course or racetrack may be worst for the street are important. Experimenting with your car's handling balance should only be done under safe, controlled conditions away from public roads.

Hondas, by the nature of their nose-heavy, front-wheel-drive layout, tend to understeer at the limit of their cornering abilities. Understeer means that when you turn the steering wheel the car turns less than you expect or continues straight ahead. It's true that Hondas are among the best handling front-wheel-drive cars built; they have precise, responsive steering and do not understeer to excess. But understeer is still the ultimate result in most circumstances.

Oversteer, on the other hand, is the at-the-limit result for some cars of different layout, particularly rear- and mid-engined cars. Oversteer is when you turn the steering wheel and the car turns more than you expect or spins out, turning backward.

It's plain that in an evasive maneuver understeer is preferable to oversteer. When a car understeers, the turned front tires scrub off speed as if they were being braked. If room is available, the car slows enough for the tires to regain traction and allow the driver to evade the obstacle. In contrast, once an oversteering car skids into a broadslide or spins, it is out of control and solely in the hands of fate.

The problem is that some oversteer can be an advantage under the relatively predictable circumstances of a race or autocross course. The driver knows where the turns or slaloms are, and can prepare to correct when the tail of the car slides wide. The driver then has the advantage of a car that turns into corners quickly and scrubs off little speed when turning.

A car driven on the street should retain understeer at its cornering limit. Otherwise, avoiding an unexpected obstacle could put the car into a spin; there would be no time to plan steering corrections to compensate for the oversteer. One other note: A car whose handling feels neutral or oversteers lightly on a low-speed autocross course may oversteer heavily at highway speeds. If you race or autocross a street-driven car, and set it up to oversteer, either change the settings to understeer before heading out on the street, or keep the car off the street and trailer it.

Most importantly, adjustments that change handling balance must not be tested on the street. The experimentation must take place on a race course or autocross course, preferably during a practice session. Make just one adjustment at a time in order to be sure which change causes what effect. The best plan is to start out with baseline settings and log your times through the course and the results of any other tests you may make. Make a change and log its results. Then go back to the baseline settings and test again. The second set of baseline results should be the same as the first. This ensures that no variables such as changes in the road surface are affecting the test.

With these things in mind, here are some adjustments that will add traction to the end of the car at which they are made. A guideline to remember is that adding traction at the front of the car increases oversteer; adding traction at the rear increases understeer.

• Higher tire pressure will increase cornering traction. However, there is a point at which increased air pressure will cause the tire to bulge across the tread. When the tread rounds out like this, its contact patch and traction decrease. Except for racing or autocrossing, do not exceed the maximum pressure recommended for the tire.

• A certain amount of negative camber, depending on the tires and car, will increase traction. Some drivers, in order to reduce understeer, will use positive camber at the rear.

• Increasing caster to the front end will increase its cornering traction. It has little effect at the rear.

• Within tire make and model, the wider the tire, the better the traction as long as it fits the wheel and car properly. To reduce understeer, a wider tire at the front makes sense, although it looks odd.

Jackson Racing, when using Yokohama 008-R tires which have a slick outer shoulder for added cornering traction, mounts the rear tires backward on its Showroom Stock race cars so that the slick section is on the inside, reducing rear traction to cut down understeer.

• Reduce or move weight. Cornering traction will increase at the end that is lightened.

• Changing from toe-in to toe-out, or increasing toe-out, will make the end of the car at which the change is made react quicker to steering inputs. The car will turn in faster. This is particularly useful in autocrossing, but can make the car prone to over-steering in street driving or high-speed driving. The car also may dart under braking.

Some adjustments produce opposite results. Spring and anti-roll bar alterations at one end of the

A more expensive but nonetheless valuable tool for measuring cornering, as well as acceleration and braking, is the G-Analyst. Grady Wood mounts a G-Analyst just to the right of the instrument pod on his CRX.

car increase traction at the other end. For instance, to reduce understeer and gain more traction at the front, add a stiffer anti-roll bar or stiffer springs at the rear. Conversely, to reduce oversteer and gain more traction at the rear, stiffen up the front with a stronger anti-roll bar or springs.

An anti-roll bar trick used by Jackson Racing that helps turn-in is loosening the front anti-roll bar connections somewhat (ensure that the bolts will not loosen further while you're running). Doing so increases the front cornering traction when the steering wheel is first turned. However, when the car rolls farther, the anti-roll bar comes into play, shifting some of the cornering traction to the rear.

Stiffening the rear shocks has much the same effect. The car turns in quickly because of the traction shifted forward by this added rear-suspension resistance. But once the car settles into the corner, the shock absorbers' influence diminishes, shifting cornering traction rearward again. As you would expect, stiffening the front shocks has the opposite effect, increasing understeer initially and eventually having little effect on the handling balance until the car changes direction again.

Measuring suspension tune

The effects of tire pressure, camber, caster and tire size can be measured several ways. The simplest method is to buy a bottle of white liquid shoe polish. Mark a stripe across the inside and outside shoulders of the tires. The mark should be about two inches long, extending onto the tread a bit as well as the sidewall. Run the car on the race or autocross course, or a skid pad. When you finish, look at the marks. Each of the adjustments should be balanced so that the white is scuffed off all the tread but not any of the sidewall.

A more technical way to accomplish the same thing is to measure the tire temperature with a pyrometer immediately after leaving the track. Measure all four tires at the outside, middle and inside of the tread. Change the adjustments to make the readings as even as possible.

There are also several devices sold that measure cornering force. One of the most common is the G-Analyst. It reads lateral acceleration, forward acceleration and braking, and displays the results on an electronic graph. This approach is valuable in

The most sophisticated measuring tools are out of the financial reach of many enthusiasts. Here, a 1989 Civic Si is run through a test autocross course by *Grassroots Motorsports* magazine. The unit mounted to the hood and front bumper of the car is used for timing acceleration and measuring braking distances; it works optically, independent from any other attachments. A smaller sensor on the right-rear fender reads reflections from track-side reflecting boards; an on-board computer records the segment times between the reflectors.

measuring overall cornering traction. And analyzing the car's cornering ability at the beginning, middle and end of various corners can reveal much about its handling balance and ability to turn in. An accessory for the G-Analyst allows its data to be transmitted to a personal computer, making a valuable log for recording different adjustments and their effects.

If the car were ideal, all four tires would corner flatly and run at the same pressure, providing neutral handling. With Honda's front-wheel drive and heavy front ends, that cannot be achieved. However, this ideal can be approached—closely in competition and with a substantial safety margin on the street—by careful suspension tuning.

9

Consider all the options

There are a number of popular accessories for sporting Hondas that have less effect on performance than mechanical modifications and adjustments. Some, like body kits, are primarily intended to make the car look better, but may reduce aerodynamic drag as well. Others, like sports seats, are mostly aimed at comfort, although they may improve control during hard cornering by helping to restrain the driver. And some, like racing-type gauges, allow the driver to monitor the engine more exactly. These parts are worthwhile because they round out a high-performance Honda, making it look and feel the part of a sports coupe or sports sedan, in addition to acting the part.

Aerodynamic modifications
Air dams

Air dams are among the more functional body add-ons available. They not only lend a low-to-the-ground look to the front end, but they also can reduce aerodynamic drag and lift, and can carry driving lights and oil coolers.

Air dams came out of sports car racing where their main purpose was to control airflow at the front

The A-T Engineering air dam on the author's Civic 1200 raised the oil temperature during steady highway driving by 20 degrees. While that's not desirable, it is an indication of how much air it diverted from the underside of the engine and car. Doing so can significantly reduce a car's aerodynamic drag. The oil temperature was lowered with an oil cooler.

Angelo Roberson used the full Jackson Racing IMSA body kit for his Civic 1200. It includes air dam and front and rear fender flares. Missing from Roberson's car is the front gravel panel. The kit can be bonded on or riveted.

of the car. The operation of these racing-oriented air dams is much like that of a water dam, only inverted. While a conventional dam keeps water from flowing over its banks onto the surrounding land, an air dam keeps air from flowing under its lip and swirling underneath the car. Instead, the dam diverts the air around the car.

The idea is to move as much of the air down the relatively smooth sides of the car rather than underneath the chassis. The bottom of the chassis is cluttered with wind-catching components like the engine, transaxle and suspension. Damming the space underneath the front end improves the car's aerodynamics, allowing it to slip through the air with less effort. A second benefit is reduction of aerodynamic lift by keeping air from bunching up under the front of the car. This wave of air lifts the front end of the car just like a boat rises on its bow wave. The result, of course, is much more subtle with air because it is not nearly as dense as water, but the effect is comparable. Reducing lift is important because lift lessens the weight on the tires, cutting their contact with the road and their ability to corner and brake.

The addition of a deep A-T Engineering air dam to an *Auto-X* magazine Civic 1200 project car raised the oil temperature by 20 degrees Fahrenheit at constant highway speeds. The temperature increase gives an idea of how much air had been washing past the oil pan before the air dam was installed. The higher oil temperature was undesirable, of course, and was lowered by adding an air cooler. But the aerodynamic improvement was worth the oil-cooler trade-off.

Air dams can be good mounting points for several accessories. Among them are driving lights, particularly fog lights because they can be mounted low. That way their beams are well below eye level, reducing glare and passing underneath fog that hovers just above the road. An oil cooler can be mounted in some air dams as well. The mounting of lights or coolers may require custom bodywork to cut the openings and fabricate sturdy mountings. Also, any oil cooler mounted low on a car should be protected with heavy screening to keep rocks from puncturing it.

Rear spoilers

A rear spoiler—a lip or small inverted wing at the end of the trunk lid or on the trailing edge of a hatchback's roof—can be functional as well. While it may not lower the car's aerodynamic drag greatly or may increase it slightly, a spoiler also can reduce aerodynamic lift. It goes about this in a different way than an air dam, but can be just as effective.

As a car drives through the air, the air flows over the hood, windshield and top, following these surfaces fairly closely. But because of the rear window's steep angle, the air separates from the car there, trailing downward at a lesser angle. The void between this billowing sheet of air and the trunk lid creates an area of low pressure, lifting the rear end upward. A spoiler works by sticking up into the airstream and grabbing some of the passing air, creating high pressure at the end of the car and helping to press it to the road.

A secondary benefit from some spoilers is reduced drag. By reaching up and reattaching the airflow to the car, drag-inducing turbulence behind the car can be reduced. On the other hand, some spoilers divert so much air that they increase drag. That may be a desirable trade-off if the car is used for racing on a course with tight turns and short straightaways.

Mounting a spoiler usually is easy. A few holes may have to be drilled through the trunk lid for retaining bolts, or the spoiler may attach to the top of the hatch. If the spoiler is to match the body's color, it must be painted. But, generally, no other bodywork is required.

Body kits

Good body kits take artfully sculpted air dams and rear spoilers, and add flared moldings for the rocker panels and lower wheelwells to make just about any Honda or Acura look lower, wider and sportier. The best kits will do this in a way that smooths turbulence around the wheelwells, reduces

Fender flares are available in kit form from Jackson Racing for either serious track use or style on the street. These flares are made from handlaid fiberglass and bolt on to early 1500 Civics. The kit also includes the front spoiler. *Jackson Racing*

The Jackson Racing side skirt kit is made from reinforced fiberglass, and bolts on to the 1984–87 CRX models. The

Pulsar wheels are also available from Jackson. *Jackson Racing* lift front and rear, and reduces overall aerodynamic drag.

While it's a personal and fairly easy matter to decide which kit looks the best for a particular model, it's difficult to determine which is aerodynamically best, or will fit well and hold up the longest. When possible, talk to others who have bought body kits. Don't limit yourself to Honda owners, because few body kits are made by companies that specialize just in Hondas; most companies build kits for a wide range of marques. Reputation for quality is important, so give weight to brand names; Kaminari and Kamei are examples for aerodynamic kits and parts.

If you can, look at an unassembled kit. The surfaces should be smooth and the edges should be finished. Make sure that the method of attachment is sturdy. And read the instructions to see what work is

Preludes can be dressed up for the street. This is Jackson Racing's three-piece body kit for 1988–89 two-liter Preludes. *Jackson Racing*

Jackson Racing also makes body kits for the Integra and Legend. The kits include front air dams, side skirts and rear valances—all manufactured from fiberglass and ready to bolt on. *Jackson Racing*

Mugen offers body kits for street Hondas, including this fiberglass kit for the CRX. Others are available for the Civic and Integra. *King Motorsports*

involved. If you can't see the kit beforehand, ask the distributor to mail you a photocopy of the instructions.

Often, installing a body kit and painting it to match your car is best left to a specialist. Remember that many photos in catalogs are of carefully massaged cars, prepared specifically for photographing. If you have a specialist or body shop install the kit, ask to see samples of previous installations, and ask whether the sample car was completely repainted or if just the body kit was painted.

Wheels, suspension and lowering kits

While many look at high-performance wheels as a way to reduce unsprung weight, mount larger, better-handling tires or improve brake cooling, there's plenty to be said for choosing a set of wheels that simply improves a car's appearance. In doing so, your stylistic taste should be your guide. Just be sure that the wheels you choose will mount tires of a size that makes sense for your Honda, that they will mount on the brake hubs snugly and that they have the proper offset so that handling won't be upset.

Suspension kits that lower the car are looked at in the same vein by some; they sharpen the handling but more importantly, they make the car look sharp. When reasoning in this form-over-function manner, be sure to consider what the car will be used for. If the car is intended for show or will be used on smooth, flat desert highways, then ground clearance won't be much of a concern. On the other hand, if the car will be used on potholed city streets, on bumpy

mountain roads or gravel forest paths, think twice about reducing ground clearance. One good whack against a rock will instantly pound the most smoothly bent header into something as useful and attractive as a squashed beer can.

Oil coolers and accumulators

All Honda engines rely on two fluids for longevity: coolant (a mixture of water and ethylene glycol antifreeze) and oil. While both are important, the coolant serves just one purpose: it draws heat from the engine. Oil, on the other hand, pulls double duty, lubricating the engine and pitching in on the cooling duties. This secondary cooling is further complicated by many Honda models that run the exhaust system directly underneath the oil pan, radiating extra heat into the oil. The additional heat can cause the oil to break down and lose its ability to lubricate. Dealing with this dilemma is often a job just for race mechanics, but it should be a consideration for many street-driven high-performance Hondas as well.

The solution for an engine with hot oil—more than 250 degrees Fahrenheit—is an oil cooler, a miniature radiator for the oil. It should be mounted at the front of the car in the airstream. Some kits attach the cooler to the front of the radiator, others leave it up to the owner to search out the best location and fabricate mountings. If the oil runs marginally hot without a cooler or if the car is raced in a class that doesn't allow an oil cooler, consider synthetic oil because most brands of synthetic oil will tolerate much higher temperatures than conventional oil.

An oil cooler can make a big difference for certain Hondas, particularly those like the Civic 1200 in which the exhaust swoops directly underneath the oil pan, adding heat to the oil within. This arrangement on the author's Civic uses an adaptor on the stock oil filter mount, a remote-mounted oil filter and a large cooler in the vacant area behind the grille, to the left of the radiator.

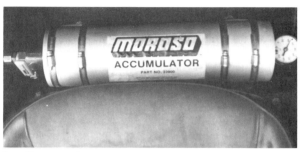

An oil accumulator can help Hondas that lose oil pressure during hard cornering. Again, the Civic 1200 is a good example. Because of the closeness of the exhaust system, there is no room to enlarge the oil pan and there is little room inside for baffles. This Moroso accumulator is mounted in front of the passenger's seat in the author's Civic and holds three quarts of oil. When the oil pressure drops below the reading on the air pressure gauge, left, the air works against a piston inside to force oil through the output line, right, and into the engine, keeping the oil pressure up.

The accumulator's pressure line runs just in front of the driver's seat, along the left side of the driver's footwell and into the engine compartment, through the firewall. There, it is connected to the output hose from the oil filter with a tee. A check valve in the oil filter keeps the oil from running the wrong direction when the accumulator comes into play.

The engine's oil cooler is mounted in the front air dam of the ex-King Motorsports tube-frame Integra. Air is channeled directly into the face of the cooler through the fiberglass air dam's venting, while the stainless steel oil lines are conveniently routed through the tube framing. *G. William Krause*

Another oil problem that appears under certain conditions in Hondas, particularly racing, is low oil pressure when cornering. An oil accumulator can be the savior for Hondas that are cornered hard enough to produce oil starvation and low oil pressure. This occurs when cornering forces the oil away from the oil pump's pickup. The pump sucks up air, oil pressure plummets and crankshaft bearings become endangered.

Traditionally, tuners have solved this problem by adding baffles to the pan. These small oil dams keep the oil from sloshing from side to side. However, in some Honda cases, because of rules or because of exhaust routing and limited oil pan size, baffles cannot be added. That was the case with the *Auto-X* magazine Civic 1200 project car. It had been

lowered, used a four-into-one tube header, was street-driven, and there was no room to add baffles or enlarge the pan. Under those conditions an oil accumulator was the best option.

An accumulator is an aluminum cylinder with a piston inside. One end of the cylinder is plumbed through an on-off valve into the engine's oil system with an oil filter adaptor. The other end has a valve that allows it to be pressurized with air using a tire-inflation hose. So, on one side of the piston is oil and on the other is air.

Once installed, the accumulator is charged with air to move the piston to the oil end of the cylinder.

All but a few pounds of air is then bled off. The engine is started and the oil valve is opened. The oil fills the cylinder, moving the piston toward the air end. As the piston moves, it compresses the air. When the air pressure equals the oil pressure, the accumulator is ready to use. The oil valve is shut, the engine is turned off and the crankcase is topped off with oil. The car is raced with the oil valve open.

If the oil pressure drops, the air pressure pushes the piston toward the oil end of the accumulator, forcing oil into the engine and restoring most of the oil pressure. When the car exits the corner and the oil pump pickup is fully immersed again, the pump recharges the accumulator, moving the piston back toward the air end and recompressing the air.

An oil accumulator provides one other advantage. By opening the oil valve before starting the engine, oil can flow through the bearings and other components before the engine is started. Wait for the oil pressure gauge to rise and then start the engine which already is pressurized with oil. As soon as the engine is running, the oil pump recharges the accumulator.

Road lighting

Improved headlights can be added to many Hondas, and fog lights and driving lights can be

Even the headlights of many Hondas can be improved with the addition of high-quality lights like this Cibie high beam for a second-generation Accord. The lead-crystal lens allows the light pattern to be more precisely aimed than with standard glass. The replaceable quartz-halogen bulb can be bought in various outputs for street or competition use.

added to all Hondas. Hondas that use standard-sized headlights can benefit from high-performance headlights; Hondas like the 1986 and later Civics and CRXs that use aerodynamically faired-in headlights are not included.

Most high-performance headlights are made in Europe, use a separate quartz-halogen bulb that plugs into the headlight reflector and lens (rather than being sealed into a single assembly), and use a lead crystal lens instead of the common glass used in standard or quartz-halogen sealed-beam headlights. The better glass allows a lens design that spreads the bulb's light more evenly and precisely. And the two-part construction allows the use of high-output bulbs for rallying, night racing or on the highway in states where they're allowed.

Driving lights

Driving lights come with reflectors and lenses for various purposes. The most common is for fog; in fact these driving lights are more commonly called fog lights. A fog light's beam is wide and flat. It throws little light upward into fog or rain, limiting glare.

The next most common is the standard driving light. It has a much narrower and longer range pattern to augment the high-beam headlights.

The least common driving light pattern, but one that makes a lot of sense for backroad driving and racing, is the pencil beam. The pencil-beam driving light gets its name from the long and thin beam it throws ahead of the car. Its beam is much longer than a high-beam headlight's, but its concentration of brightness is most annoying to oncoming traffic. So it's best used on lonely backroads, or long racetrack or rally straightaways.

Wiring

Replacement headlights with high-power bulbs require relays and heavier wiring because of the extra current drawn by their brighter bulbs. Relays are available from light suppliers; 12 or 14 gauge wire, and crimp-on wire connectors can be bought at auto supply and hardware stores. When hand wiring headlights, be sure to use fuses. Some relays have the fuses built in. If not, include an in-line fuse for each circuit.

The same applies for driving lights. Use 12 or 14 gauge wire, and either high-current switches or switches and relays, and make sure each circuit has a fuse.

To figure the current requirements in amperes for a relay or fuse, divide the bulb's wattage by 12 volts. Many light manufacturers make this simpler by selling a pair of driving lights with a kit that includes a switch, relay, fuse and wiring harness.

Interior modifications
Seats

Generally, only the seats in the Integra, Prelude and Si Hondas are intended for sporting use. High-performance seats differ from standard seats by having larger, stiffer bolsters—wings that wrap around the driver's or passenger's torso, hips and thighs to provide greater restraint during hard cornering. A driver who's using the steering wheel as a grab handle to keep from sliding out of the seat will have trouble steering precisely. The difference in steering control between a car with a standard seat and an identical car with a high-performance seat can be astounding to someone who's never made such a comparison. In an accident, a seat's strength and design can be important because its frame must avoid collapse which can worsen injuries.

The attachment of the seat to the car is just as important as the seat itself. Look for seats that offer mounting kits that are both sturdy and provide full adjustment. When choosing high-performance seats,

High-output headlights or driving lights require relays, heavy-duty wiring and individual fuses. This relay, right, taps into the main accessory fuse on a 1982 Civic through an additional in-line fuse (white, center), and is used to power 100 watt high beams.

The interior of Bob Endicott's CRX shows how the addition of a few components can make the car easier to control during hard cornering. He uses a racing seat, seat belt harness and a small-diameter, thick rimmed steering wheel.

consider a name brand. The better known seats are often better constructed; Recaro seats are well-regarded, for instance, although they're expensive. Beyond reputation for engineering and strength, look for high-quality upholstery that's well-fitted. Some seat companies offer their upholstery material in bulk for recovering the back seat or door panels to match; that may be a consideration when outfitting an interior.

Racing seats have become popular on the street as well as on the track. They provide the ultimate in support and restraint, and have a more purposeful look. Further, they usually have slots cut in them for five-point racing seatbelts. The disadvantages of using a racing seat include no seatback adjustments, and the need for custom brackets that must be well-designed and properly installed.

Steering wheels

The steering wheel is the driver's most important link to the car. Its rim must fit the driver's hands, offer good grip and be sized for quick response. The size is important because each inch of hand movement turns a smaller wheel farther than a larger wheel.

Of course, there are practical limits to using smaller steering wheels. First, a small wheel will be too hard to turn; the driver won't have sufficient leverage. Second, a production car with upright seating needs a larger steering wheel than a formula car with a lie-down seat; the arms must bend at a comfortable angle. Third, a small wheel will block the driver's view of the tachometer, speedometer and other gauges. Usually, this means choosing a wheel that's no more than one to two inches smaller than stock.

Gauges

Accessory gauges may not make a car faster, but they can help a knowledgeable driver protect an engine from damage or troubleshoot tuning problems. When looking at gauges, there are three general choices to make: size, needle sweep and mechanical operation versus electrical operation.

The most common gauge diameter is 2 in., while some mini gauges of 1⅜ in. diameter are sold for cars with limited dashboard space, and gauges of 2⅝ in. diameter are popular for racing. The bigger the gauge's face, the more exact and quicker to read it will be. This is the reason for the popularity of 2⅝ in.

To shift weight to the rear of the car, Bob Endicott remounted the battery behind the passenger compartment in a plastic storage box.

gauges among race drivers. In general, it makes sense to choose the largest size that will fit the space available.

Look for gauges with 270 degrees of needle sweep (nearly the full circumference of the gauge). Gauges with restricted sweeps are less-exact and harder-to-read; they use a small portion of their faces and are no better than smaller gauges with greater sweeps.

Mechanical gauges work regardless of electrical problems and can be quite accurate. But they also can be fragile, particularly a temperature gauge, which uses a thin capillary tube filled with ether. The tube connects the temperature sensor to the gauge. Capillary tubes are somewhat flexible but still can be snapped off easily, ruining the gauge.

Electric gauges generally are easier to install, needing only a wire or two each, rather than a cumbersome capillary tube or pressure tube. They also can be quite accurate, but work only when the key is on and battery voltage is within the proper range. For newer Hondas this is no worry because the engine computer has the same electrical requirements. If the charging system fails and the battery discharges, the car won't run anyway.

Tachometers

A tachometer is a must in all high-performance cars, and ought to be included in all manually shifted cars regardless of performance level. A tach is important because it identifies the maximum engine speed for upshifting, and because it can show up tuning

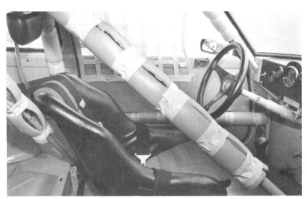

This is the interior of a car intended for a single purpose: racing. Angelo Roberson's Civic has a racing seat and steering wheel, a hand-fabricated metal dashboard with the appropriate gauges; everything else has been removed to save weight. A roll cage and window net have been added for safety.

George Cleveland's Civic 1200 uses the tachometer from a Civic CVCC five-speed which moves the gas and water-temperature gauges into separate pods in the middle of the dashboard. The racing seat and thickly padded steering wheel and shift knobs make the interior a pleasant place for spirited driving.

problems when the engine is unwilling to run strongly throughout the rpm range.

Relatively few Hondas have come without tachometers; all Honda lines have offered tachs at one option level or another. So, for a Honda with no tachometer, searching junkyards for a factory tach makes sense. Most are mechanical, driven by a cable connected to the camshaft through a special adaptor. And usually the other gauges are rearranged. This means that the engine adaptor, cable and the affected gauges and wiring should be bought along with the tachometer. While this approach results in the cleanest installation, it may not be the easiest.

There are two other, easier to install options. The first is a mechanical accessory tachometer that uses a universal mounting bracket for installation on the dashboard or steering column. For this, a cable adaptor for the engine is usually required, making the other option, an electric accessory tachometer, the simplest to install. Electric tachs come in a wide range of sizes and also use a universal mount.

Try to avoid using the steering column as a mounting platform. But if you have no other choice, be sure there is substantial clearance between the steering wheel and the front of the tach, and the back of the tach and the dashboard. The clearance is needed in case of an accident to leave room for the steering column to collapse. An improperly mounted tach can jam the column, resulting in serious chest or head injuries. If you cannot find a suitable mounting point, search out the factory components and use them.

Oil gauges

Since most Hondas come equipped with tachometers, the addition of an oil pressure gauge is usually considered first. Honda commonly uses a light to indicate low oil pressure but does not include a gauge. The acceptable range varies from engine to engine, so consult your service manual. But, generally, a Honda engine should produce 40 to 50 pounds per square inch of oil pressure at highway speeds and 15 to 20 psi at idle.

Another oil-related gauge that may be overkill for the street but is vital for racing is an oil temperature gauge. The gauge usually takes readings from oil in the bottom of the oil pan, and can show when an oil cooler is needed (more than 250 degrees Fahrenheit), or when bearing or other friction-causing problems crop up. A bearing that is going bad will make the oil temperature rise sharply. Shutting off the engine quickly could limit damage to just one or two components, while continued use could lead to a blown engine.

Installing an oil temperature gauge can be difficult if you have to remove the oil pan, cut a hole for

The supplementary gauges are 2⅝ in. racing gauges from Auto Meter. They measure water temperature, oil pressure and oil temperature. These readings are normal after a hard run.

The author took a different instrumentation approach on his Civic 1200, mounting a tachometer on the steering column, and a trio of supplementary mechanical gauges on the center of the dash.

Finding a place to install a sensor for an oil temperature gauge can be difficult. The author drilled the oil pan and brazed in an adaptor while the engine was apart for a rebuild.

the sensor and weld in an adaptor. Some gauges come with a kit for installing the sensor in the drain plug, which is much easier.

Fuel pressure gauges

For racers using carbureted engines, a fuel pressure gauge is good for keeping an eye on fuel delivery at the top of the rpm range and toward the end of long straightaways, when insufficient fuel flow most often occurs.

If you install a mechanical fuel pressure gauge, as most are, place it outside the car. Mount it in a pod on the cowl, because such gauges use a tube that taps into the fuel line and routes pressurized fuel directly into the gauge. The whole assembly should be outside of the driver's compartment in case of an accident that severs the tube, causing a fuel leak.

An alternative is an Auto Meter fuel pressure gauge, which uses an isolating diaphragm under the hood. In this case, the pressurized fuel is routed through a tube to one side of a diaphragm, housed in a metal case. Isolated from the fuel on the other side of the diaphragm is a second tube, filled with a mixture of ethylene glycol and water (the same mixture as engine coolant). This column of non-flammable antifreeze runs to the gauge, transmitting the fuel's pressure indirectly to the mechanical gauge. As the fuel pressure rises, the fuel presses harder on the isolating diaphragm. The diaphragm in turn presses against the column of antifreeze which increases pressure within the gauge, moving its needle. Because the line leading to the gauge contains no fuel, the gauge may be mounted inside the driver's compartment.

Other gauges

Water temperature gauges are commonly found on Hondas but they don't read out in degrees. They just indicate a normal range, and whether the engine is relatively cold, at normal temperature or hot. A high-performance gauge allows the water temperature to be read in one- or two-degree increments.

Either an ammeter to show the alternator's output, or a voltage gauge to show the battery's charge and the voltage regulator's operation, will allow the driver to keep a closer watch on the electrical system.

Any car using a turbocharger should have a boost/vacuum gauge to read out the pressure produced by the turbo; many turbo kits include such gauges.

Safety equipment

In the same way that a thorough complement of gauges is as much at home in a race car as in a show car or sports car, so is high-performance safety equipment. Quite a bit of this equipment is required for road racing, including roll bars or roll cages, racing-type seatbelt harnesses and a fire extinguisher. Each component can be used on the street as well, if properly installed. Understanding their functions helps in deciding which ones make the most sense outside a racetrack.

Roll bars and cages

A roll bar is made from tubular steel. It is shaped like an upside-down U, and fits just behind the driver's and passenger's seats. The bar helps to keep the roof from collapsing if the car rolls over. The ends of the U's legs are welded to flanges that bolt through the floor to matching plates on the bottom of the floor pan; this part of the bar provides most of the protection. Two braces run rearward and, depending on the car and the bar, attach to the tops of the rear wheelwells or to the floor toward the rear of the car. These braces help keep the bar from being bent forward or backward in a rollover. A diagonal member runs from the top of the U on one side of the car to the bottom of the car on the other side. This brace helps to keep the brace from bending side to side.

A roll cage is a roll bar with a front section added that increases crash protection. To create a roll cage, another upside-down U hoop is added at the front of the driver's compartment. Its shape closely follows that of the roof and its front pillars. The front hoop attaches to the floor near the front of the door. Left- and right-handed bars run over the doors to attach the front and rear hoops to one another. Usually, a dashboard-high brace runs from side to side, between the legs of the forward hoop. And, in some designs, bars at mid-door level connect the hoops to provide strength if the car is hit from the side.

The benefits of a roll bar or roll cage are simple: The car is more sturdy in case of a wreck. Additionally, a bar or cage makes the unibody chassis stiffer, giving the suspension a firmer base to work against. The disadvantages are the weight, the room taken up and, for some roll cages, the difficulty of getting in and out of the car.

Seatbelts

Racing seatbelt harnesses contain 3 in. wide lap belts that are about an inch wider than standard belts, a submarine belt that runs downward from the central belt buckle to the floor and keeps the lap belt from riding up on the torso, and two shoulder belts. These belts can provide greater protection than standard belts if installed properly and used religiously. They are much harder to adjust and buckle than standard belts, however, leading some to use them only occasionally or only in part. In that case, the easy-to-use standard belts provide better protection because they're more likely to be used.

Fire extinguishers

Fire extinguishers make sense in all cars, sports and otherwise. For most cases, an inexpensive dry chemical extinguisher is sufficient. The chemical powder is hard to remove, however. Halon fire extinguishers are somewhat more expensive but do not use hard-to-clean dry chemicals. Instead, they use a gas vapor that extinguishes flames. In either case, a solid, metal bracket should be used to mount the extinguisher. Most plastic mounts are meant for hanging extinguishers from walls, and would allow an extinguisher to break loose and fly dangerously through the driver's compartment during hard maneuvering or an accident.

Conclusion

Even if appearance is the only motivation for adding air dams or wheels, the shiny aluminum of an oil accumulator or cooler, the bright brass of an oil control valve, or the sparkle of stainless steel hose braiding, there are performance reasons for these components as well. So, remember to map out performance goals, and then consider all the options. Think through the purposes and abilities of each component. Use it only if it will help meet your goal, and fit and look like a factory installation. Insist both on performance and style. That's what Honda does.

Appendix

Civic
First generation, Civic 1973–79
Engine bore and stroke
1200:
'73	70x76 mm
'74–79	72x76 mm
CVCC:
'75–79	74x86.5 mm

Displacement
1200:
'73	1170 cc
'74–79	1237 cc
CVCC:
'75–79	1488 cc

Compression ratio
1200:
'73	8.3:1
'74–79	8.1:1
CVCC:
'75 2-door and 3-door	8.1:1
'75 wagon	7.7:1
'76–79	7.9:1

Carburetion
1200:
'73–76	Hitachi two-barrel
'77–79	Keihin two-barrel
CVCC:
'75–79	Keihin three-barrel

Power
1200:
'73	50 hp @ 5000 rpm
'74–77	52 hp @ 5000 rpm
'78–79	55 hp @ 5000 rpm
CVCC:
'75 2-door and 3-door	53 hp @ 5000 rpm
'76	60 hp @ 5000 rpm
'77	60 hp @ 5000 rpm
'78–79	63 hp @ 5000 rpm

Torque
1200:
'73	59 lb-ft @ 3000 rpm
'74–76	60.5 lb-ft @ 4000 rpm
'77	65 lb-ft @ 2000 rpm
78–79	67 lb-ft @ 2500 rpm
CVCC:
'75 2-door and 3-door	68 lb-ft @ 3000 rpm
'76	76 lb-ft @ 3000 rpm
'77–79	77 lb-ft @ 3000 rpm

Transaxle
'73–77 1200 4-speed:
First-gear ratio	3.000:1
Second-gear ratio	1.789:1
Third-gear ratio	1.182:1
Fourth-gear ratio	0.846:1
Final-drive ratio	4.933:1

'78–79 1200 4-speed:
First-gear ratio	3.181:1
Second-gear ratio	1.823:1
Third-gear ratio	1.181:1
Fourth-gear ratio	0.846:1
Final-drive ratio	4.642:1

'75 CVCC 4-speed and 5-speed, 2-door and 3-door:
First-gear ratio	3.000:1
Second-gear ratio	1.736:1
Third-gear ratio	1.130:1
Fourth-gear ratio	0.778:1
Fifth-gear ratio	0.655:1*
Final-drive ratio	4.733:1

'75 CVCC 4-speed and 5-speed, wagon:
First-gear ratio	3.000:1
Second-gear ratio	1.789:1
Third-gear ratio	1.182:1
Fourth-gear ratio	0.846:1
Fifth-gear ratio	0.655.1*
Final-drive ratio	4.733:1

'76 CVCC 4-speed and 5-speed:
First-gear ratio	3.181:1
Second-gear ratio	1.823:1
Third-gear ratio	1.181:1

Fourth-gear ratio	0.846:1
Fifth-gear ratio	0.714:1*
Final-drive ratio	
2-door and 3-door	4.266:1
Wagon	4.733:1
5-speed, serial number 2500001 and up	4.066:1

'77-79 CVCC 4-speed and 5-speed:

First-gear ratio	3.181:1
Second-gear ratio	1.823:1
Third-gear ratio	1.181:1
Fourth-gear ratio	0.846:1
Fifth-gear ratio	0.714:1*
Final-drive ratio	
2-door and 3-door, except Calif. and high altitude	3.875:1
2-door and 3-door Calif. and high altitude	4.428:1
Wagon	4.066:1

Weight

1200:

'73 2-door	1,536 lb.
'73 3-door	1,552 lb.
'74 2-door	1,605 lb.
'74 3-door	1,621 lb.
'75-76 2-door	1,683 lb.
'75-76 3-door	1,716 lb.
'77 2-door	1,665 lb.
'77 3-door	1,687 lb.
'78-79 2-door	1,663 lb.
'78-79 3-door	1,696 lb.

CVCC:

'75 2-door/ 4-speed	1,748 lb.
'75 3-door/ 4-speed	1,781 lb.
'75 3-door/ 5-speed	1,801 lb.
'76 2-door/ 4-speed	1,758 lb.
'76 3-door/ 4-speed	1,791 lb.
'76 3-door/ 5-speed	1,797 lb.
'77-79 2-door/ 4-speed	1,762 lb.
'77-79 3-door/ 4-speed	1,795 lb.
'77-79 3-door/ 5-speed	1,801 lb.

Wheelbase	86.61 in.
Front track	51.18 in.
Rear track	50.39 in.

Length

1200:

'73	139.76 in.
'74	146.85 in.
'75-77	147.83 in.
'78-79	145.50 in.

CVCC:

'75-77	150.00 in.
'78-79	148.60 in.

Width	59.25 in.

Height

1200:

'73-74	52.95 in.
'75-76	52.95 in.
'77	52.17 in.
'78-79	52.40 in.

CVCC:

'75-76	52.17 in.
'77-79	52.40 in.

Steering turns, lock-to-lock

1200:

'73-79	3.1

CVCC:

'73-79 2-door and 3-door	3.1
'75-76 wagon	3.1
'77-79 wagon	3.5

Note: Unless indicated otherwise, figures are for 2-door sedan and three-door hatchback models.
*Five-speed only.

Civic
Second generation, 1980-83

Engine bore and stroke

1300	72x82 mm
1500	74x86.5 mm

Displacement

1300	1335 cc
1500	1488 cc

Compression ratio

1300:

'80	7.9:1
'81	8.8:1
'82-83	9.3:1

1500:

'80, except Calif.	9.0:1
'80, Calif.	8.9:1
'81	8.8:1
'82-83	9.3:1

Carburetion	Keihin three-barrel

Power

1500:

'80-83	67 hp @ 5000 rpm

Torque

1500:

'80-81	79 lb-ft @ 3000 rpm
'82-83	79 lb-ft @ 3500 rpm

Transaxle

'80 1300 4–speed and 5–speed:

First-gear ratio	2.916:1
Second-gear ratio	1.764:1
Third-gear ratio	1.181:1
Fourth-gear ratio	0.807:1
Fifth-gear ratio	0.655:1*
Final-drive ratio	4.933:1

'80 1500 4–speed and 5–speed:

First-gear ratio	2.916:1
Second-gear ratio	1.764:1
Third-gear ratio	1.181:1
Fourth-gear ratio	0.846:1
Fifth-gear ratio	0.714:1*
Final-drive ratio	3.875:1

'81 1300 4–speed and 5–speed:

First-gear ratio	2.916:1
Second-gear ratio	1.764:1
Third-gear ratio	1.181:1
Fourth-gear ratio	0.846:1
Fifth-gear ratio	0.714:1*
Final-drive ratio	4.428:1

'81 1500 5–speed:

First-gear ratio	2.916:1
Second-gear ratio	1.764:1
Third-gear ratio	1.181:1
Fourth-gear ratio	0.846:1
Fifth-gear ratio	0.714:1*
Final-drive ratio	4.428:1

'82–83 1300 4–speed and 5–speed:

First-gear ratio	3.272:1
Second-gear ratio	1.666:1
Third-gear ratio	1.041:1
Fourth-gear ratio	0.777:1
Fifth-gear ratio	0.655:1*
Final-drive ratio	
4-speed	4.066:1
5-speed	3.722:1

'82–83 1500 5–speed:

First-gear ratio	3.181:1
Second-gear ratio	1.823:1
Third-gear ratio	1.181:1
Fourth-gear ratio	0.846:1
Fifth-gear ratio	0.714:1*
Final-drive ratio	3.875:1

Weight

'80 1300 4-speed	1,722 lb.
'80 1300 5-speed	1,736 lb.
'80 1500 4-speed, except Calif.	1,780 lb.
'80 1500 4-speed, Calif.	1,786 lb.
'80 1500 5-speed, except Calif.	1,794 lb.
'80 1500 5-speed, Calif.	1,800 lb.
'81 1300 4-speed	1,747 lb.
'81 1300 5-speed	1,753 lb.
'81 1500 5-speed, except Calif., high altitude and GL	1,812 lb.
'81 1500 5-speed, Calif. and high altitude	1,822 lb.
'81 1500 GL 5-speed	1,830 lb.
'82 1300 4-speed	1,761 lb.
'82 1300 5-speed	1,795 lb.
'82 1500 5-speed, except GL	1,854 lb.
'82 1500 GL 5-speed	1,865 lb.
'83 1300 4-speed	1,773 lb.
'83 1300 5-speed	1,803 lb.
'83 1500 5-speed, except GL and S	1,867 lb.
'83 1500 5-speed, GL and S	1,898 lb.

Wheelbase	88.6 in.
Front track	53.5 in.
Rear track	
'80	53.9 in.
'81–83	54.3 in.
Length	
'80–81	148.0 in.
'82–83	148.4 in.
Width	62.2 in.
Height	
'80–81	53.0 in.
'82–83	53.2 in.

Steering turns, lock-to-lock

'80–81	3.3
'82–83	3.6

Note: Unless indicated otherwise, figures are for hatchback models.
Five-speed only.

Civic and CRX
Third generation, 1984–87

Engine bore and stroke

1300	74x78 mm
1500	74x86.5 mm

Displacement

1300	1342 cc
1500	1488 cc

Compression ratio

1300:

'84–87	10.0:1

1500:

'84	9.2:1
'85 base CRX	9.6:1
'85–87 CRX HF	9.6:1
'85 CRX Si	8.7:1
'85 Civic	9.2:1
'86–87 CRX except HF and Si, and Civic except Si	9.2:1
'86–87 CRX Si, Civic Si	8.7:1

Carburetion

1300:

'84–87	Keihin three-barrel

1500:

'84	Keihin three-barrel
'85 except CRX Si	Keihin three-barrel
'85 CRX Si	Honda PGM-FI electronic port fuel injection
'86–87 except CRX Si, Civic Si	Keihin three-barrel
'86–87 CRX Si, Civic Si	Honda PGM-FI electronic port fuel injection

Power

1300:

'84–87	60 hp @ 5500 rpm

1500:

'84	76 hp @ 6000 rpm
'85 except CRX Si	76 hp @ 6000 rpm
'85–87 CRX HF	58 hp @ 4500 rpm
'85 CRX Si	91 hp @ 5500 rpm
'86–87 CRX Si, Civic Si	91 hp @ 5500 rpm
'86–87 except Si	76 hp @ 6000 rpm

Torque

1300:

'84–87	73 lb-ft @ 3500 rpm

1500:

'84	84 lb-ft @ 3500 rpm
'85 except CRX Si	84 lb-ft @ 3500 rpm
'85–87 CRX HF	79 lb-ft @ 2500 rpm
'85 CRX Si	93 lb-ft @ 4500 rpm
'86–87 CRX Si, Civic Si	93 lb-ft @ 4500 rpm
'86–87 except Si	84 lb-ft @ 3500 rpm

Transaxle

'84–85 4-speed 1300 Civic:

First-gear ratio	3.272:1
Second-gear ratio	1.666:1
Third-gear ratio	1.041:1
Fourth-gear ratio	0.777:1
Final-drive ratio	3.722:1

'84 1300 and 1500 5-speed CRX and Civic:

First-gear ratio	2.916:1
Second-gear ratio	1.764:1
Third-gear ratio	1.181:1
Fourth-gear ratio	0.846:1
Fifth-gear ratio	0.714:1
Final-drive ratio	
1300 CRX	3.473:1
1500 CRX and Civic S	4.266:1
1500 Civic	4.066:1

'84–85 5-speed Civic wagon:

First-gear ratio	3.181:1
Second-gear ratio	1.823:1
Third-gear ratio	1.181:1
Fourth-gear ratio	0.846:1
Fifth-gear ratio	0.714:1
Final-drive ratio	4.266:1

'85 5-speed CRX and Civic except HF and wagon:

First-gear ratio	2.916:1
Second-gear ratio	1.764:1
Third-gear ratio	1.181:1
Fourth-gear ratio	0.846:1
Fifth-gear ratio	0.714:1
Final-drive ratio	
CRX except HF and Si	4.266:1
CRX Si	4.428:1
Civic standard	4.066:1

Civic S and
4-door   4.266:1

'85 5-speed CRX HF except Calif. and
high altitude:
- First-gear ratio   3.272:1
- Second-gear
  ratio   1.666:1
- Third-gear
  ratio   1.041:1
- Fourth-gear
  ratio   0.807:1
- Fifth-gear ratio   0.714:1
- Final-drive
  ratio   2.954:1

'85 5-speed CRX HF, Calif. and high
altitude:
- First-gear ratio   2.916:1
- Second-gear
  ratio   1.526:1
- Third-gear
  ratio   0.960:1
- Fourth-gear
  ratio   0.750:1
- Fifth-gear ratio   0.655:1
- Final-drive
  ratio
  - High altitude   4.066:1
  - Calif.   3.576:1

'85 5-speed Civic wagon:
- First-gear ratio   3.181:1
- Second-gear
  ratio   1.823:1
- Third-gear
  ratio   1.181:1
- Fourth-gear
  ratio   0.846:1
- Fifth-gear ratio   0.714:1
- Final-drive
  ratio   4.266:1

'86 5-speed CRX:
- First-gear ratio   2.916:1
- Second-gear
  ratio   1.764:1
- Third-gear
  ratio   1.181:1
- Fourth-gear
  ratio   0.846:1
- Fifth-gear ratio   0.714:1
- Final-drive
  ratio
  - CRX except
    HF and Si   4.266:1
  - CRX Si   4.428:1

'86 5-speed CRX HF except Calif. and
high altitude:
- First-gear ratio   3.272:1
- Second-gear
  ratio   1.666:1
- Third-gear
  ratio   1.041:1
- Fourth-gear
  ratio   0.807:1
- Fifth-gear ratio   0.714:1
- Final-drive
  ratio   2.954:1

'86 5-speed CRX HF, Calif. and high
altitude:
- First-gear ratio   2.916:1

- Second-gear
  ratio   1.526:1
- Third-gear
  ratio   0.960:1
- Fourth-gear
  ratio   0.750:1
- Fifth-gear ratio   0.655:1
- Final-drive
  ratio
  - High altitude   4.066:1
  - Calif.   3.578:1

'86 4-speed Civic:
- First-gear ratio   3.272:1
- Second-gear
  ratio   1.666:1
- Third-gear
  ratio   1.041:1
- Fourth-gear
  ratio   0.777:1
- Final-drive
  ratio   4.266:1

'86 5-speed Civic 1500 except wagon:
- First-gear ratio   2.916:1
- Second-gear
  ratio   1.764:1
- Third-gear
  ratio   1.192:1
- Fourth-gear
  ratio   0.866:1
- Fifth-gear ratio   0.718:1
- Final-drive
  ratio
  - Except DX,
    Si, Calif.,
    high
    altitude
    and 4-door   3.578:1
  - DX   4.062:1
  - Si   4.400:1
  - Calif.   3.722:1
  - High altitude   4.266:1
  - 4-door   3.933:1

'86 5-speed Civic wagon:
- First-gear ratio   3.181:1
- Second-gear
  ratio   1.823:1
- Third-gear
  ratio   1.192:1
- Fourth-gear
  ratio   0.866:1
- Fifth-gear ratio   0.718:1
- Final-drive
  ratio   4.250:1

'87 5-speed CRX except HF:
- First-gear ratio   2.916:1
- Second-gear
  ratio   1.764:1
- Third-gear
  ratio   1.192:1
- Fourth-gear
  ratio   0.866:1
- Fifth-gear ratio   0.712:1
- Final-drive
  ratio   3.933:1

'87 5-speed CRX HF except Calif. and
high altitude:
- First-gear ratio   3.272:1

Second-gear
ratio   1.666:1
Third-gear
ratio   1.041:1
Fourth-gear
ratio   0.807:1
Fifth-gear ratio   0.655:1
Final-drive
ratio   2.954:1

'87 5-speed CRX HF, Calif. and high
altitude:
First-gear ratio   2.916:1
Second-gear
ratio   1.526:1
Third-gear
ratio   0.960:1
Fourth-gear
ratio   0.750:1
Fifth-gear ratio   0.655:1
Final-drive
ratio
High altitude   4.066:1
Calif.   3.578:1

'87 4-speed Civic except Calif.:
First-gear ratio   3.272:1
Second-gear
ratio   1.666:1
Third-gear
ratio   1.041:1
Fourth-gear
ratio   0.777:1
Final-drive
ratio   4.266:1

'87 4-speed Civic Calif.:
First-gear ratio   3.272:1
Second-gear
ratio   1.666:1
Third-gear
ratio   1.041:1
Fourth-gear
ratio,   0.750:1
Final-drive
ratio   4.266:1

'87 5-speed Civic 1500 except wagon:
First-gear ratio   2.916:1
Second-gear
ratio   1.764:1
Third-gear
ratio   1.192:1
Fourth-gear
ratio   0.866:1
Fifth-gear ratio   0.718:1
Final-drive
ratio
Except DX,
Si, Calif.,
high
altitude
and 4-door   3.578:1
DX   4.062:1
Si   4.400:1
Calif.   3.722:1
High altitude   4.266:1
4-door   4.250:1

'87 5-speed Civic wagon:
First-gear ratio   3.181:1
Second-gear
ratio   1.823:1

Third-gear
ratio   1.192:1
Fourth-gear
ratio   0.866:1
Fifth-gear ratio   0.718:1
Final-drive
ratio   4.250:1

Weight
CRX:
'84 1300   1,713 lb.
'84 1500   1,803 lb.
'85–86 except
HF and Si   1,819 lb.
'85–87 HF   1,713 lb
'85 Si   1,883 lb.
'86 Si   1,953 lb.
'87 except HF
and Si   1,865 lb.
'87 Si   1,978 lb.
Civic:
'84 1300
4-speed   1,797 lb.
'84 1500 DX
5-speed   1,863 lb.
'84 1500 S
5-speed   1,907 lb.
'85 1300
4-speed   1,837 lb.
'85 1500 DX
5-speed   1,910 lb.
'85 1500 S
5-speed   1.956 lb.
'86 1300
4-speed   1,797 lb.
'86 1500 DX
5-speed   1.958 lb.
'86 1500 Si
5-speed   2,033 lb.
87 1300
4-speed   1,887 lb.
87 1500 DX
5-speed   1,958 lb.
'87 1500 Si   2,033 lb.

Wheelbase
CRX   86.6 in.
Civic   93.7 in.
Front track
CRX and Civic   55.1
Rear track
CRX and Civic   55.7 in.
Length
CRX:
'84–85   144.7 in.
'86–87 except
Si   144.7 in.
'86–87 Si   147.8 in.
Civic:
'84–85   150.0 in.
'86–87   151.4 in.
Width
CRX and Civic   63.9 in.
Height
CRX   50.8 in.
Civic   52.6 in.
Steering turns, lock-to-lock
'84 CRX 1300,
Civic 1300   3.65

'84 CRX 1500,
  Civic 1500   4.01
'85 CRX HF,
  Civic 1300   3.55
'85–87 CRX
  base and Si,
  and Civic
  1500   3.89
'85–87 CRX
  HF,
  Civic 1300   3.55

Note: Unless indicated otherwise, Civic figures are for hatchback models.

Civic and CRX
Fourth generation, 1988–
Engine bore and stroke
1500   75x84.5 mm
1600   75x90 mm
Displacement
1500   1493 cc
1600   1590 cc
Compression ratio
'88–89 CRX HF   9.6:1
'88–89 CRX Si,
  Civic 4WD
  wagon   9.1:1
'88–89 CRX, Civic
  except Si and HF 9.2:1
Carburetion
'88–89 CRX HF and
  Si, and Civic
  4WD wagon   Honda PGM-FI
                  electronic port
                  fuel injection

'88–89 CRX, Civic
  except Si, HF
  and 4WD wagon   Honda PGM-FI
                  electronic
                  throttle-body
                  (dual-point) fuel
                  injection

Power
'88–89 CRX HF   62 hp @ 4500 rpm
'88 CRX Si, Civic
  4WD wagon   105 hp @ 6000 rpm
'88–89 Civic base
  hatchback   70 hp @ 5500 rpm
'88 base CRX, Civic
  except base
  hatchback   92 hp @ 6000 rpm
'89 CRX Si, Civic
  Si, Civic 4WD
  wagon   108 hp @ 6000 rpm
'89 base CRX, Civic
  except base
  hatchback and Si 92 hp @ 6000 rpm
Torque
'88–89 CRX HF   90 lb-ft @ 2000 rpm
'88 CRX Si, Civic
  4WD wagon   98 lb-ft @ 5000 rpm
'88–89 Civic base
  hatchback   83 lb-ft @ 3000 rpm
'88 base CRX, Civic
  except base
  hatchback   89 lb-ft @ 4500 rpm

'89 CRX Si, Civic
  Si, Civic 4WD
  wagon   100 lb-ft @ 5000 rpm
'89 base CRX, Civic
  except base
  hatchback
  and Si   89 lb-ft @ 4500 rpm

Transaxle
'88 5-speed CRX and Civic, except CRX
  HF:
    First-gear ratio   3.250:1
    Second-gear
      ratio   1.894:1
    Third-gear
      ratio   1.259:1
    Fourth-gear
      ratio   0.937:1
    Fifth-gear ratio   0.771:1
    Final-drive
      ratio
      CRX base
        model   3.722:1
      CRX Si   4.250:1
      Civic hatch-
        backs   3.722:1
      Civic 4-door   4.058:1
'88–89 5-speed CRX HF:
    First-gear ratio   3.250:1
    Second-gear
      ratio   1.650:1
    Third-gear
      ratio   1.033:1
    Fourth-gear
      ratio   0.823:1
    Fifth-gear ratio   0.694:1
    Final-drive
      ratio
      Except Calif.   2.954:1
      Calif.   3.250:1
'88–89 4-speed Civic base hatchback:
    First-gear ratio   3.250:1
    Second-gear
      ratio   1.650:1
    Third-gear
      ratio   1.033:1
    Fourth-gear
      ratio   0.823:1
    Final-drive
      ratio   3.888:1
'88–89 5-speed Civic wagon 2WD:
    First-gear ratio   3.250:1
    Second-gear
      ratio   1.894:1
    Third-gear
      ratio   1.259:1
    Fourth-gear
      ratio   0.937:1
    Fifth-gear ratio   0.771:1
    Final-drive
      ratio   4.058:1
'89 5-speed CRX and Civic, except CRX
  HF:
    First-gear ratio   3.250:1
    Second-gear
      ratio   1.894:1
    Third-gear
      ratio   1.259:1

Fourth-gear
 ratio 0.937:1
Fifth-gear ratio 0.771:1
Final-drive
 ratio
CRX base
 model 3.888:1
CRX Si 4.250:1
Civic
 hatchbacks
 except Si 3.888:1
Civic Si 4.250:1
Civic 4-door 4.058:1

Weight
'88 base CRX 1,922 lb.
'88 CRX HF 1,819 lb.
'88 CRX Si 2,017 lb.
'88 Civic hatchback 1,935 lb.
'89 base CRX 2,048 lb.
'89 CRX HF 1,834 lb.
'89 CRX Si 2,138 lb.
'89 Civic hatchback 2,018 lb.
'89 Civic Si 2,161 lb.

Wheelbase
'88–89 CRX 90.6 in.
'88–89 Civic 98.4 in.

Front track
'88–89 CRX, Civic
 except wagons 57.1 in.

Rear track
'88 CRX, Civic
 except wagons 57.1 in.
'89 CRX, Civic
 except wagons 57.3 in.

Length
'88–89 CRX 147.8 in.
'88–89 Civic
 hatchbacks 156.1 in.

Width
'88–89 CRX 65.7 in.
'88–89 Civic
 hatchbacks 65.6 in.

Height
'88 CRX 50.0 in.
'88 Civic
 hatchbacks 52.4 in.
'89 CRX 50.1 in.
'89 Civic
 hatchbacks 52.5 in.

Steering turns, lock-to-lock
'88 CRX 3.87
'88 Civic
 hatchbacks 3.87
'88 Civic power 3.65
'89 CRX Si 4.1
'89 CRX manual 3.8
'89 CRX variable 4.8
'89 Civic
 hatchbacks 3.87
'89 Civic variable 4.1
'89 Civic power 3.65

Accord
First generation, 1977–81
Engine bore and stroke
'77–78 74x93 mm
'79–81 77x94 mm

Displacement
'77–78 1597 cc
'79–81 1751 cc

Compression ratio
'77–81 8.0:1

Carburetion
'77–81 Keihin three-barrel

Power
'77–78 68 hp @ 5000 rpm
'79 72 hp @ 4500 rpm
'80–81 68 hp @ 4500 rpm

Torque
'77–78 85 lb-ft @ 3500 rpm
'79 94 lb-ft @ 3000 rpm
'80–81 94 lb-ft @ 2500 rpm

Transaxle
'77 5-speed:
 First-gear ratio 3.18:1
 Second-gear
  ratio 1.82:1
 Third-gear
  ratio 1.18:1
 Fourth-gear
  ratio 0.84:1
 Fifth-gear ratio 0.71:1
 Final-drive
  ratio 4.26:1
'78 5-speed:
 First-gear ratio 3.18:1
 Second-gear
  ratio 1.82:1
 Third-gear
  ratio 1.18:1
 Fourth-gear
  ratio 0.84:1
 Fifth-gear ratio 0.71:1
 Final-drive
  ratio 4.12:1
'79 5-speed:
 First-gear ratio 3.18:1
 Second-gear
  ratio 1.84:1
 Third-gear
  ratio 1.20:1
 Fourth-gear
  ratio 0.90:1
 Fifth-gear ratio 0.72:1
 Final-drive
  ratio 4.38:1
'80–81 5-speed:
 First-gear ratio 3.18:1
 Second-gear
  ratio 1.84:1
 Third-gear
  ratio 1.20:1
 Fourth-gear
  ratio 0.90:1
 Fifth-gear ratio 0.72:1
 Final-drive
  ratio 3.58:1

Weight
'77–78 2,018 lb.
'79 2,203 lb.
'80 2,239 lb.
'81 2,240 lb.

Wheelbase
'77–81 93.7 in.

Front track

'77–78	55.1 in.
'79–81	55.5 in.

Rear track

'77–78	54.7 in.
'79–81	55.1 in.

Length

'77–78	162.8 in.
'79	163.2 in.
'80–81	171.9 in.

Width

'77–81	63.8 in.

Height

'77–78	52.4 in.
'79	52.6 in.
'80–81	53.3 in.

Steering turns, lock-to-lock

'77–78	3.2
'79–81	3.5

Note: Unless indicated otherwise, 1977–79 figures are for hatchback and 1980–81 figures are for four-door.

Accord
Second generation, 1982–85

Engine bore and stroke

'82–83	77x94 mm
'84–85	80x91 mm

Displacement

'82–83	1751 cc
'84–85	1829 cc

Compression ratio

'82–83	8.8:1
'84	9.0:1
'85 SEi	8.8:1
'85 except SEi	9.0:1

Carburetion

'82–84	Keihin three-barrel
'85 SEi	Honda PGM-FI electronic port fuel injection
'85 except SEi	Keihin three-barrel

Power

'82–83	75 hp @ 4500 rpm
'84	86 hp @ 5500 rpm
'85 SEi	101 hp @ 5800 rpm
'85 except SEi	86 hp @ 5800 rpm

Torque

'82–83	96 lb-ft @ 3000 rpm
'84	99 lb-ft @ 3500 rpm
'85 SEi	108 lb-ft @ 2500 rpm
'85 except SEi	99 lb-ft @ 3500 rpm

Transaxle

'82 3-speed automatic:

First-gear ratio	2.38:1
Second-gear ratio	1.56:1
Third-gear ratio	0.97:1
Final-drive ratio	3.59:1

'83 4-speed automatic:

First-gear ratio	2.38:1
Second-gear ratio	1.56:1
Third-gear ratio	1.03:1
Fourth-gear ratio	0.78:1
Final-drive ratio	3.59:1

'84 5-speed manual:

First-gear ratio	3.18:1
Second-gear ratio	1.84:1
Third-gear ratio	1.20:1
Fourth-gear ratio	0.87:1
Fifth-gear ratio	0.68:1
Final-drive ratio	4.07:1

'85 5-speed manual:

First-gear ratio	3.18:1
Second-gear ratio	1.84:1
Third-gear ratio	1.20:1
Fourth-gear ratio	0.87:1
Fifth-gear ratio	0.68:1
Final-drive ratio	3.87:1

Weight

'82 4-door	2,185 lb.
'83 4-door	2,200 lb.
'84 hatchback	2,270 lb.
'85 SEi 4-door	2,465 lb.
'85 hatchback	2,235 lb.

Wheelbase

'82–85	96.5 in.

Front track

'82–83	56.3 in.
'84–85	56.9 in.

Rear track

'82–85	55.9 in.

Length

'82–83 4-door	173.6 in.
'84 hatchback	175.4 in.
'85 SEi 4-door	175.4 in.
'85 hatchback	167.5 in.

Width

'82	65.0 in.
'83	65.4 in.
'84	65.6 in.
'85 SEi 4-door	65.6 in.
'85 hatchback	65.2 in.

Height

'82–84	54.1 in.
'85 SEi 4-door	54.1 in.
'85 hatchback	53.3 in.

Turning circle

'82	36.7 ft.
'83–85	34.1 ft.

Steering turns, lock-to-lock

'82–83 4-door	3.1
'84 hatchback	2.8
'85 SEi 4-door	2.8
'85 hatchback	3.5

Accord
Third generation, 1986–

Engine bore and stroke

'86–89	82.7x91 mm

Displacement

'86–89	1955 cc

Compression ratio

'86–87	8.8:1
'88–89 DX, LX	9.1:1
'88–89 LXi	9.3:1

Carburetion

'86–89 DX, LX	Keihin two-barrel
'86–89 LXi	Honda PGM-FI electronic port fuel injection

Power

'86–89 DX, LX	98 hp @ 5500 rpm
'86–87 LXi	110 hp @ 5500 rpm
'88–89 LXi	120 hp @ 5800 rpm

Torque

'86–89 DX, LX	109 lb-ft @ 3500 rpm
'86–87 LXi	114 lb-ft @ 4500 rpm
'88–89	122 lb-ft @ 4000 rpm

Transaxle

'86–89 DX, LX 5-speed:

First-gear ratio	3.18:1
Second-gear ratio	1.84:1
Third-gear ratio	1.21:1
Fourth-gear ratio	0.88:1
Fifth-gear ratio	0.69:1
Final-drive ratio	3.87:1

'86–89 LXi 5-speed:

First-gear ratio	3.18:1
Second-gear ratio	1.84:1
Third-gear ratio	1.21:1
Fourth-gear ratio	0.88:1
Fifth-gear ratio	0.69:1
Final-drive ratio	4.07:1

Weight

'86 DX hatchback	2,415 lb.
'86–87 LXi 4-door	2,565 lb.
'88–89 DX hatchback	2,513 lb.
'88 LXi hatchback	2,685 lb.
'88 DX coupe	2,493 lb.
'88–89 LXi coupe	2,646 lb.
'88 DX 4-door	2,482 lb.
'88 LXi 4-door	2,668 lb.
'89 LXi hatchback	2,641 lb.
'89 DX coupe	2,493 lb.
'89 DX 4-door	2,500 lb.
'89 LXi 4-door	2,685 lb.

Wheelbase

'86–89	102.4 in.

Front track

'86–89	58.3 in.

Rear track

'86–89	58.1 in.

Length

'86–89 hatchback	174.8 in.
'86–87 4-door	178.5 in.
'88–89	179.7 in.

Width

'86–89 hatchback	66.7 in.
'86–89 except hatchback	67.4 in.

Height

'86–89 hatchback	52.6 in.
'86–87 4-door	53.3 in.
'88–89 4-door	53.4 in.
'89 coupe	52.7 in.

Steering turns, lock-to-lock

'86–89 hatchback	3.1
'86–89 4-door	3.1
'88–89 coupe	3.1

Prelude
First generation, 1980–83

Engine bore and stroke — 77x94 mm

Displacement — 1751 cc

Compression ratio

'80–81	8.0:1
'82–83	8.8:1

Carburetion — Keihin three-barrel

Power

'80–81	72 hp @ 4500 rpm
'82–83	75 hp @ 4500 rpm

Torque

'80–81	94 lb-ft @ 3000 rpm
'82–83	96 lb-ft @ 3000 rpm

Transaxle

'80–81 5-speed:

First-gear ratio	3.18:1
Second-gear ratio	1.84:1
Third-gear ratio	1.20:1
Fourth-gear ratio	0.90:1
Fifth-gear ratio	0.72:1
Final-drive ratio	4.38:1

'82–83 5-speed:

First-gear ratio	3.18:1
Second-gear ratio	1.94:1
Third-gear ratio	1.29:1
Fourth-gear ratio	0.90:1
Fifth-gear ratio	0.72:1
Final-drive ratio	4.07:1

Weight

'80–81	2,130 lb.
'82–83	2,140 lb.

Wheelbase

'80–83	91.3 in.

Front track

'80–83	55.1 in.

Rear track

'80–83	55.5 in.

Length

'80–83	161.4 in.

Width

'80–83	64.4 in.

Height

'80–83	51.0 in.

Steering turns, lock-to-lock

'80	3.3
'81–83	3.2

Prelude
Second generation, 1984–87

Engine bore and stroke

'84–85	80x91 mm
'86–87 2.0 Si	82.7x91 mm

Displacement

'84–85	1829 cc
'86–87 2.0 Si	1955 cc

Compression ratio

'84–85	9.1:1
'86–87 2.0 Si	8.8:1

Carburetion

'84–85	Two Keihin sidedraft constant-velocity one-barrel
'86–87 2.0 Si	Honda PGM-FI electronic port fuel injection

Power

'84–85	100 hp @ 5500 rpm
'86–87 2.0 Si	110 hp @ 5500 rpm

Torque

'84	107 lb-ft @ 4000 rpm
'85	104 lb-ft @ 4000 rpm
'86–87 2.0 Si	114 lb-ft @ 4500 rpm

Transaxle

'84–85 5-speed:

First-gear ratio	3.18:1
Second-gear ratio	1.94:1
Third-gear ratio	1.25:1
Fourth-gear ratio	0.93:1
Fifth-gear ratio	0.76:1
Final-drive ratio	4.07:1

'86 5-speed 2.0 Si:

First-gear ratio	3.18:1
Second-gear ratio	1.94:1
Third-gear ratio	1.25:1
Fourth-gear ratio	0.93:1
Fifth-gear ratio	0.76:1
Final-drive ratio	4.07:1

'87 5-speed 2.0 Si:

First-gear ratio	3.18:1
Second-gear ratio	1.84:1
Third-gear ratio	1.21:1
Fourth-gear ratio	0.88:1
Fifth-gear ratio	0.69:1
Final-drive ratio	4.07:1

Weight

'84–85	2,265 lb.
'86–87 2.0 Si	2,380 lb.

Wheelbase

'84–87	96.5 in.

Front track

'84–87	57.9 in.

Rear track

'84–87	57.9 in.

Length

'84–85	169.1 in.
'86–87 2.0 Si	172.0 in.

Width

'84–85	66.5 in.
'86–87 2.0 Si	66.9 in.

Height

'84–85	51.0 in.
'86–87 2.0 Si	48.6 in.

Steering turns, lock-to-lock

'84–85	2.8
'86–87 2.0 Si	2.8

Prelude
Third generation, 1988–

Engine bore and stroke

'88–89	81x95 mm

Displacement

'88–89	1958 cc

Compression ratio

'88–89 S	9.1:1
'88–89 Si	9.0:1

Carburetion

'88–89 S	Two Keihin sidedraft constant-velocity one-barrel
'88–89 Si	Honda PGM-FI electronic port fuel injection

Power

'88–89 S manual transaxle	104 hp @ 5800 rpm
'88–89 S automatic transaxle	105 hp @ 5800 rpm
'88–89 Si	135 hp @ 6200 rpm

Torque

'88–89 S, manual and automatic transaxle	111 lb-ft @ 4000 rpm
'88–89 Si	127 lb-ft @ 4500 rpm

Transaxle

'88 5-speed:

First-gear ratio	3.17:1
Second-gear ratio	1.86:1
Third-gear ratio	1.26:1
Fourth-gear ratio	0.94:1
Fifth-gear ratio	0.79:1
Final-drive ratio	
S	4.19:1
Si	4.06:1

'89 S 5-speed:

First-gear ratio	3.25:1
Second-gear ratio	1.86:1

Third-gear
ratio 1.26:1
Fourth-gear
ratio 0.94:1
Fifth-gear ratio 0.79:1
Final-drive
ratio 4.19:1
'89 Si 5-speed:
First-gear ratio 3.17:1
Second-gear
ratio 1.86:1
Third-gear
ratio 1.26:1
Fourth-gear
ratio 0.94:1
Fifth-gear ratio 0.79:1
Final-drive
ratio 4.27:1

Weight
'88 S 2,573 lb.
'88 Si 2,665 lb.
'89 S 2,571 lb.
'89 Si 2,712 lb.
Wheelbase
'88 101.0 in.
'89 101.1 in.
Front track
'88–89 58.3 in.
Rear track
'88–89 57.9 in.
Length
'88–89 175.6 in.
Width
'88–89 67.3 in.
Height
'88–89 51.0 in.
Steering turns, lock-to-lock
'88–89 S, Si except
4WS 2.84
'88–89 Si 4WS 2.66

Integra
First generation, 1987–89
**Engine bore and
stroke** 75x90 mm
Displacement 1590 cc
Compression ratio
'87 9.3:1
'88–89 9.5:1

Carburetion Honda PGM-FI
electronic port
fuel injection
Power
'87 113 hp @ 6250 rpm
'88–89 118 hp @ 6500 rpm
Torque
'87 99 lb-ft @ 5500 rpm
'88–89 103 lb-ft @ 5500
rpm
Transaxle
'87–89 5-speed:
First-gear ratio 3.18:1
Second-gear
ratio 1.94:1
Third-gear
ratio 1.34:1
Fourth-gear
ratio 1.03:1
Fifth-gear ratio 0.84:1
Final-drive ratio 4.21:1
Weight
3-door:
'87 2,326 lb.
'88–89 2,313 lb.
Wheelbase
3-door:
'87–89 96.5 in.
5-door:
'87–89 99.2 in.
Front track
'87–89 55.9 in.
Rear track
'87–89 56.5 in.
Length
'87 168.5 in.
'88–89 168.7 in.
Width
'87 64.9 in.
'88–89 65.6 in.
Height
'87–89 52.9 in.
Steering turns, lock-to-lock
'87 3.6
'88–89 3.5

Note: Unless indicated otherwise, figures
are for three-door RS.

Sources

There are a handful of companies around the United States that specialize in high-performance Hondas. These tuning houses develop, manufacture and distribute high-performance parts for Hondas. Most of their business is done through mail-order catalogs, although many also have shops at or near their headquarters where they will make modifications for customers. Following is a list of the major Honda specialists, as well as three other companies whose work is also of interest to Honda enthusiasts.

A-T Engineering
2 Candlewood Lake Road North
New Milford, Connecticut 06776

A-T Engineering claims to be the longest-running Honda tuner in the United States. Founded in 1977 by Serge Harabosky, a former science teacher, Harabosky's company offers a wide range of components for all Hondas, beginning with the first Civic and continuing through the current Hondas and Acuras. Included in A-T's lineup are appearance accessories, aerodynamic body parts, brake components, carburetors, clutches, driving lights, flywheels, engine components, headers and exhaust systems, interior components, racing parts, suspension components and wheels. A-T also prepares Hondas for racing in its shop.

Cartech Inc.
11212 Goodnight Lane
Dallas, Texas 75229

Cartech specializes in turbocharging; it manufactures systems for a number of makes and models. Two of its systems are designed for Hondas: the first fits the 1985–87 CRX Si; the second fits the 1988–89 CRX Si. A-T Engineering is a dealer for the latter Cartech system, and has built a project car with suspension and body components that complement it. Cartech was founded in 1977 by the company's chief, Corky Bell.

CRE/Performance
Rt. 122 Worcester Road
Barre, Massachusetts 01005

CRE/Performance is known by this preferred name, and two other monikers: Chuck's Racing Enterprises and Chuck's Civic Center. It all boils down to the same thing, though: Chuck Noonan's shop. Noonan came to national attention when he won the Sports Car Club of America's national autocrossing championship in C Street Prepared three times straight in his CRX, starting in 1984. CRE/Performance has remained active in autocrossing, winning additional championships since. Among the products it offers are brake components, carburetors, clutches, engine components, headers and exhaust systems, interior components, racing parts, suspension components and wheels. CRE/Performance specializes in the 1984–87 Civic and CRX, although it works on other Hondas, and makes special Honda and Acura conversions at its shop.

HKS USA Inc.
20312 Gramercy Place
Torrance, California 90501

HKS USA's roots are in Japan, where its parent company manufactures high-performance parts for many Japanese cars. HKS USA develops its prototypes in California on US specification Japanese cars; the parts are then produced in Japan from these prototypes and shipped to the United States. The company develops and sells turbocharging systems, exhaust systems, engine components, flywheels and ignition systems for Hondas and Acuras. The company has concentrated on the first-generation Integra, second-generation Prelude, and third-generation Civic and CRX.

Jackson Racing
16291 Gothard Street
Huntington Beach, California 92647

Jackson Racing is one of the larger and more-active Honda tuners. Founded in 1979 by the company's chief, Oscar Jackson, the company is heavily involved in racing, having won SCCA national road racing and endurance championships, and autocrossing and rallying championships, among others. Jackson Racing offers race car preparation through its shop and, through its catalog, a wide array of components for nearly all Hondas—from the first Civic through the current Hondas and Acuras. Included are appearance accessories, aerodynamic body parts, brake components, carburetors, clutches, driving lights, engine components, flywheels, headers and exhaust systems, interior components, limited-slip differentials, racing parts, suspension components and wheels.

King Motorsports
105 East Main Street
Sullivan, Wisconsin 53178

King Motorsports is an outgrowth of a Honda dealership—King Honda of Milwaukee—that was also known for its racing Hondas. Founder Jim Denticci has won SCCA national road racing championships in his Hondas, and the company prepares race cars out of its shop. King Motorsports is the US importer for the Mugen Company of Japan. (Mugen is pronounced Moo-gen, with a hard G and the second syllable rhyming with hen.) Mugen was founded and is headed by Hirotoshi Honda, son of Honda Motor Company founder Soichiro Honda. Among the Mugen parts offered are appearance accessories, aerodynamic body parts, brake components, carburetors, clutches, driving lights, engine components, flywheels, headers and exhaust systems, interior components, limited-slip differentials, racing parts, suspension components, close-ratio transaxles and gear sets, and wheels.

RC Engineering
1728 Border Avenue
Torrance, California 90501

Russ Collins founded RC Engineering in the early 1970s to augment his motorcycle drag racing. Collins became well-known in motorcycle circles—he holds the National Hot Rod Association's quarter-mile speed record for the retired Top Fuel Motorcycle class at 199 mph, which he set in 1978 on a motorcycle powered by two Honda 750 engines. In 1984, RC moved into automotive-engine building, with Honda a natural specialty (the company builds other makes of engines as well). SCCA endurance racing championships came quickly, and RC has held a reputation as a top Honda engine builder since.

Shankle Automotive Engineering Inc.
9135-F Alabama Avenue
Chatsworth, California 91311

John Shankle's Shankle Automotive Engineering has been in the high-performance and racing business longer than any of the other Honda tuners, but did not offer Honda products until 1987. Shankle, who started racing Alfa Romeos in 1959, opened his business in 1967 as an Alfa Romeo specialist, racing-engine developer and builder, and suspension developer. Included in Shankle's Lightspeed product line—which concentrates on 1984 and later Hondas and Acuras—are appearance accessories, aerodynamic body parts, brake components, carburetors, driving lights, engine components, headers and exhaust systems, interior components, racing parts, suspension components and wheels.

Index